MW01060086

The
Flight
of the
Phoenix

The
Flight
of the
Phoenix

Thoughts on
Work and Life

SAMUEL H. HOWARD

Providence House Publishers

PROVIDENCE PUBLISHING CORPORATION

FRANKLIN, TENNESSEE

TENNESSEE HERITAGE LIBRARY

Printed in the United States of America

11   10   09   08   07   1   2   3   4   5

Library of Congress Control Number: 2007921428

ISBN: 978-1-57736-379-8

Cover and page design by Joey McNair
Cover photo by Roger Vando

PROVIDENCE HOUSE PUBLISHERS
an imprint of
Providence Publishing Corporation
238 Seaboard Lane • Franklin, Tennessee 37067
www.providence-publishing.com
800-321-5692

For my mother and father,
Nellie Maud Gaines Howard
and Houston Howard

CONTENTS

Foreword by Bobby L. Lovett, PhD   ix
Acknowledgments   xvii

Prologue: Out of the Fire   3
1. Going Home   13
2. As the Twig Is Bent, So Grows the Tree   21
3. Early Years   37
4. The College of Life   53
5. Fly, Phoenix   77
6. The View from the Peak   87
7. Prison Without Bars   101
Epilogue: A Wing and a Prayer   129

Howard's Law: Rules for Work   147

FOREWORD

And finally, need I add that I who speak here am bone of the
bone and flesh of the flesh of them that live within the Veil?

—W. E. B. DuBois,
The Souls of Black Folk (1903)

*I*t would be difficult to exaggerate the importance of
business in American history. "In a private-enterprise
system, the entrepreneur—the risk-taking businessman—
is the chief protagonist and the architect of most economic
progress."[1] An entrepreneur is a person engaged in "creative
entrepreneurship," which is the primary cause of real
economic growth in the American nation.[2] Since the 1830s,
Americans have invested their abilities and capital in pursuit
of the capitalistic dream.

Especially since the formation in 1899 of the National
Negro Business League by Booker T. Washington and others,
Negroes too were engaged in that pursuit; but they were
confined by racial terminology and unfair laws that governed
race relations, thus impeding their success. In the age of Jim
Crow, Negro businessmen enjoyed an attentive clientele
within a segregated community. Following World War II
(1939–1945), America's society began to disengage Jim
Crow, opening up new opportunities and, indeed, complex
challenges for minority businessmen and entrepreneurs.

I believe, too, that the most stunning mercantile successes
at the top will continue to be men and women working as
entrepreneurs, bootstrapping money, and probing the
mysteries of economic synergism.

—Theodore Cross, *Black Capitalism*

The Flight of the Phoenix is a fascinating, well-written,
high-interest story, told from the personal experience of

American businessman and entrepreneur Samuel H. Howard. Among the strengths of the book are the use of Howard's personal story and a recounting of his trials and triumphs to expound a business philosophy. This book also may serve to develop a teaching tool for people intending to pursue corporate careers. In particular, *The Flight of the Phoenix* is a personal saga about an American citizen, a highly educated, experienced, and capable businessman, in the midst of the post–World War II New South. The story follows him while he is acquiring the skills, knowledge, and contacts, and then attempting to build a multimillion dollar corporation—not in the North and the East, but in the American South where African American aspirants to success in business face the greatest of odds.

Born on May 8, 1939, in Marietta, Oklahoma, Samuel H. Howard lived in a home without the conveniences of running water or indoor toilet. At the time, America was struggling to escape the strangling grip of the Great Depression, World War II was raising its head in Europe, and Jim Crow had been under attack for four years by the NAACP, other Negro Civil Rights leaders, and by New Deal liberals in the federal government. Within this milieu, Samuel Howard's family moved during his child-hood to Sanger, Texas, and then to Lawton, Oklahoma. Samuel Howard lived there most of his childhood, completing all his secondary education, and graduating as the valedictorian from Douglass High School in 1956. He was considered an exemplary student who served in many leadership capacities, including president of the senior class and the student council.

Notwithstanding Jim Crow's boundaries, young Samuel Howard disallowed the obstacles over which he had no control. He focused instead on his intrinsic abilities to rise above the crowd, never having lost faith in the American dream. In that Jim Crow environment, however, opportunities were grudgingly extended to Americans of color—especially to Negroes such as young Samuel Howard. American Negroes had been effectively disenfranchised in many Southern states, including Oklahoma, by 1910.

The civil rights movement began in the mid-1930s and continued through World War II, reaching its acme in the late 1940s and 1950s. *An American Dilemma*, published in 1944 by Swedish scholar Gunnar Mydral, convincingly documented how American Negroes were oppressed. In 1946 and 1947, President Harry S. Truman responded with studies on race relations, then issued executive orders forbidding discrimination and ending segregation of America's armed forces. In 1949, Ada Lois Sipuel (Fisher) sued for admission of Negroes to the traditionally all-white University of Oklahoma. In June 1950, George W. McLaurin did likewise. Both suits were successful. Negro citizens in approximately six states sued to end Jim Crow schools between 1950 and 1952, and the U.S. Supreme Court rendered a definitive decision in *Brown v. Board of Education, Topeka, Kansas*.

In this new era of integration, Samuel Howard enrolled in 1956 as the only Negro student in the College of Business at Oklahoma State University. He was elected to the Blue Key Fraternity, Delta Sigma Pi, and Business Student Council, and became a member of other campus organizations. After graduating in 1961 with a bachelor of science degree in business, he attended Stanford University as an Eichler fellow, receiving a master of arts degree in 1963.

Howard was a financial analyst with the General Electric Company from 1963 to 1966, working as a trainee in America's premier financial management training program. From 1966 to 1967, at the age of twenty-seven, he served as a White House fellow with U.S. Ambassador Arthur Goldberg at the United Nations. From 1968 to 1972, Howard held various positions with TAW International

Leasing, Inc., culminating as vice president of finance, secretary, and treasurer.

Howard founded Phoenix Communications Group, Inc., in 1972, which built KTPK-FM in Topeka, Kansas. He then owned radio stations WVOL-AM and WQQK-FM in Nashville, Tennessee, for seventeen years.

Samuel H. Howard moved to Nashville in 1973 to further his career. The height of the civil rights movement was fourteen years old by then. Over the previous thirteen years, the city had become desegregated mostly due to the sit-in demonstrations by local college students, as well as protests and boycotts by the Nashville Christian Leadership Council and others. By the time Howard arrived in the city, the Nashville Human Rights Commission had already been created and Congress had passed a series of effective Civil Rights acts. The de facto aspects of racial discrimination remained dormant but not dead, indeed, as benign racial attitudes treaded the American landscape.

Notwithstanding, Howard began his career in health care in November 1973 as vice president of finance and business at Meharry Medical College in Nashville, Tennessee. Howard joined Hospital Affiliates International, Inc. as vice president of planning in 1977, and was promoted to vice president of the INA Health Care Group in May 1979. The following year, he became vice president and treasurer of Hospital Affiliates, and then in 1981, joined Hospital Corporation of America (HCA) as vice president and treasurer. He was promoted to senior vice president of public affairs in 1988 before becoming chairman of Phoenix Holdings, Inc., in January 1989. In April 1993, he used $1 million of his personal funds to start Phoenix Health Care Corporation, making it the fourteenth-largest privately held corporation in Nashville. As Xantus, it had revenues of $300 million by 1999.

When building his career and companies, Howard maintained a commitment to social responsibility. He untiringly remained active in his community as well as the wider, integrated community of the city. He was the first African American to chair the Nashville Chamber of Commerce. He chaired the Urban League of Middle Tennessee, served as a trustee for Fisk University for ten years, was elected a member of the Nashville branch of the Federal Reserve, served on two federal commissions on health care, became a member of the National Conference of Christians and Jews, and received several awards, including Nashvillian of the Year (1988), the Nashville NAACP Image Award for Lifetime Achievement (1994), and Philanthropist of the Year (1997). Indubitably, Samuel H. Howard used his natural abilities, his extensive formal education, and his business experiences to rise to the top.

In *The Flight of the Phoenix*, Howard uses no racial crutches when detailing his rise to success in the business world. The focus is on his founding a health care management organization (HMO), Xantus Healthplan, which was a response to the state of Tennessee's establishment of a program called TennCare to replace its Medicaid program. He started Xantus with $1 million in personal loans and dreamed of taking the company into the Fortune 500. But as Tennessee began to underfund the TennCare program, it forced Xantus and other smaller HMOs to take on more uninsurable TennCare patients while allowing larger, white majority companies, like Blue Cross/Blue Shield, to drop such unprofitable patients. White officials threatened Howard with indictment for transferring $10 million from Xantus to the parent company, Xantus Corporation. Just as they would later do for another large African American HMO, Access MedPlus, state officials took over Xantus. The U.S. attorney for Middle Tennessee absolved Howard of any wrongdoing.

After Howard resigned as CEO, the Xantus Healthplan, under state management, spent millions with lawyers and consultants as the beneficiaries before it failed and closed in 2003. Many observers believed the blame really remained with Tennessee's notoriously inept administrators and the ineffective structure of the state's TennCare program, which as late as 2005, was hopelessly hundreds of millions of dollars in debt. Rather than correcting the situation by forcing the white HMOs, particularly Blue Cross, to assume the poorest and costliest patients—like the minority HMOs had been forced to do (even to the point of bankruptcy)—Tennessee dropped hundreds of thousands of these impoverished citizens from TennCare.

Lloyd Elam, former president of Meharry Medical College and an expert on health care, said, "The people who started TennCare didn't realize how complex it would be. . . . They did not apply the rules equally to all companies. It affected Sam more than his share, because Blue Cross [/Blue Shield] was permitted to stop taking uninsurable [persons], but Xantus [Healthplan] wasn't. . . ." Tellingly, state officials closed Xantus and another African American owned/operated TennCare management organization, Access MedPlus, while allowing an operation like Blue Cross/Blue Shield of Tennessee to amass one billion dollars in surplus cash by 2005.

Meanwhile, Samuel Howard was so hurt and disappointed in 2003 that he sat down to write *The Flight of the Phoenix*. His purposes included the intent to set the record straight, to clear his good name, and to point out the bureaucratic blunders that destroyed Xantus. He believed, too, that the state's action imperiled (perhaps beyond repair) the TennCare program for Tennessee's most needy citizens. In the last chapters of this book, Howard skillfully details the problems in the TennCare program that led to his company's demise.

One could easily conclude that "Bureaucrats are intolerant persons that gain power and give justification to their continued and perhaps pointless existence by creating rules, regulations, procedures, work and sweat for others to do." But their role goes further, as this author wrote in *The Civil Rights Movement in Tennessee*. It extends beyond covering governmental inefficiency and corruption; their historical role in the South has often served as a vanguard to restrict some citizens from access to entrepreneurial opportunity on the basis of class and race. These same state officials, like many whites, conceivably believed—even at the end of the twentieth-first century—that African Americans should never be allowed to become successful and wealthy in big business, particularly in a white-supremacy South.[3]

In *The Flight of the Phoenix*, however, Samuel Howard refuses to say that racism was a major cause of the failure of both his company and Access MedPlus. Howard, instead, makes the point that in order for minority entrepreneurs to achieve success in big business, they must ignore the barriers presented by race (that nagging omnipresence in America). Instead, young entrepreneurs must provide quality services and products without labels of race. Howard wrote *The Flight of the Phoenix* to encourage young people to pursue their entrepreneurial dreams. The story is about:

> overcoming, and thriving, especially for people of color, for women, for the handicapped, the disadvantaged and the young—but ultimately, it's for anyone who wants to succeed. [He also said,] Over the years, I'd suffered plenty of setbacks, including having a business go into bankruptcy. I'd emerged wiser, and eventually, wealthier than ever. I had learned long ago not to take criticism and hard luck personally.

For those who are interested in striving for success in American business despite obstacles of poverty, class, and race, *The Flight of the Phoenix* is a lesson worth learning. For academicians, it's a book containing economic history,

African American biography, and Tennessee history, as well as the ongoing struggle of minorities to achieve full participation in the American economic dream: free capitalism.

Bobby L. Lovett, PhD
Professor of History, Tennessee State University

Notes

1. C. Joseph Pusateri, *A History of American Business* (Arlington Heights, Ill.: Harlan Davidson, 1984), 3–11.

2. Joseph Schumpeter, *The Theory of Economic Development* (Oxford: Oxford University Press, 1911), preface.

3. B. L. Lovett, *The Civil Rights Movement in Tennessee* (Knoxville, Tenn.: University of Tennessee Press, 2005), vii–xxv.

ACKNOWLEDGMENTS

One thing that became clear as I worked on this book is the impact of others on my life and career. I can't begin to list every one who influenced and helped, but there are a few individuals to whom I am profoundly grateful.

I first acknowledge the love and support of Karan, my wife of forty-four years. In faith, she married an individual with no car, job, or money. She has been truly loyal and supportive of the many relocations and directions that my life has taken. I thank my two children, Anica and Buddy. They have always been helpful and supportive, particularly, leaving positions with major corporations to work with me at Xantus. I am grateful to and proud of them both.

I am also grateful to Tanya Hausmann, Georganna Husband, and Stephen Braden for their loyal and unwaivering support over the past ten years. I also thank all the employees of Xantus Corporation for their loyalty during trying times. My legal team has been most effective and valuable in its support in both the criminal and civil matters. In particular, I thank Ruth Ellis, Robert Walker, Joe Welborn, Joe Johnson, and George Lambert. I also acknowledge the contributions of Robert Ritchie (now deceased).

I appreciate the assistance of Krista Reese in the preparation of this book. Without Krista's assistance, this book would not have been produced. In traveling with me to my hometown, she captured the environment and historical context of my experiences. I am also appreciative of the staff at Providence House Publishers who helped make this book a reality. Finally, I also want to thank the contributors to this book, each of whom has had a profound impact on my life.

Phoenix, a fabulous bird connected with the worship of the sun, especially in ancient Egypt and classical antiquity . . . The phoenix . . . is large as an eagle, with brilliant scarlet and gold plumage and a melodious cry . . .

Only one phoenix exists at any time. It is very long-lived . . . As its end approaches, the phoenix fashions a nest of aromatic boughs and spices, sets it on fire, and is consumed in the flames. From this pyre miraculously springs a new phoenix . . .

Egyptians associated the phoenix with intimations of immortality . . . It is also widely interpreted as an allegory of resurrection and life after death . . .

—*Encyclopedia Britannica online,*

S.V. "Phoenix."

The
Flight
of the
Phoenix

OUT OF THE FIRE

A good name is to be chosen rather than great riches,
loving favor rather than silver and gold.

—Proverbs 22:1 (NKJV)

*O*n Saturday morning, June 26, 1999, I was alone. My
wife, Karan, was out of town, but as usual, I woke
up at 5:30, showered, dressed, and walked outside to
get the newspaper. My footsteps echoed in the big, empty
house as I carried the paper inside.

Until we'd built this home, some of our friends had
teased us about the modest one we'd lived in long after our
years of struggle had ended. In 1984, we finally built the
house we live in now—about nine thousand square feet on
three acres in Nashville's Forest Hills community. By that
time, our fortunes seemed secure, despite the ups and downs
of my entrepreneurial career.

Still, we opted for comfortable digs rather than an osten-
tatious showplace. We have a big kitchen, a family room
with a pool table, and some art that we enjoy. Later, we
installed a pool in the backyard, and more recently, a home
theater and screened porch. My kids, Buddy (Samuel II)
and Anica, couldn't believe it when their workaholic Dad
actually took time to relax and float in the pool, which I had

specified to be only five-and-a-half feet deep. I might have learned how to swim with the sharks in the business world, but I couldn't do much more than dogpaddle in a real pool.

At sixty, I was enjoying my life in a way I'd never been able to before—and cherishing recognition from my adopted hometown of Nashville. I'd been involved in the process of shaping public policy on a national level from the time I'd been chosen as a White House fellow in 1966, to my appointment by President Reagan to the 1982 Advisory Council on Social Security; and my later appointment by House Speaker Newt Gingrich to the National Bipartisan Commission on the Future of Medicare in 1998. Being acknowledged as a pillar of Nashville's business community, however, was something new.

When Karan and I arrived in Nashville in 1973, we weren't sure what to expect. Neither of us had lived in the segregated South while growing up, and even in the early '70s, Nashville's public schools were still struggling to integrate. Jefferson Street, the African American business district, didn't have a single nationally franchised restaurant. A poorly planned interstate, I-40, had divided the town, worsened white flight, and created even greater obstacles for struggling black-owned businesses, as well as for Meharry College, the historically black medical school I came to town to work for.

But we found that in 1973, Nashville had arrived at a crossroads. After the demonstrations and sit-ins of the '60s, the lingering bitterness had at last begun to clear, and integration moved forward peacefully. Businesspeople in particular had begun to take a hand in moving Nashville into the future. The city was ripe with opportunities for educated people of color. I was well-prepared to enter every door that opened before me. And as you'll see, many opened.

Besides my business successes, for which I'd earned great material rewards, in the last few years the city had honored me for my years of leadership in charitable work with Easter Seals, the National Conference of Christians and Jews, 100 Black Men, and my mentoring sessions for young entrepreneurs at Tennessee State University, among many other activities. After being selected as Philanthropist of the Year in 1997, the last in a string of several such honors, I agreed to sit for interviews that trumpeted my success and leadership, in part because I believed black businesspeople needed successful role models. I'd just completed a term as chairman of Nashville's Chamber of Commerce—the first African American elected to that position.

At the peak of my personal and professional success, however, my most profitable and high-profile venture had hit a crisis. When Tennessee adopted a visionary plan called TennCare, bringing in private enterprise to cover the state's uninsured, I'd founded a health care management corporation (HMO) called Xantus. TennCare's hybrid of state funding and free enterprise replaced its Medicaid program, stemmed rising medical costs, and provided medical insurance coverage to the uninsured in Tennessee. It was a governmental course of action I'd recommended as a member of those presidential commissions. I was convinced it was the way of the future for our nation's forty-four million uninsured.

TennCare's first few years were outstanding successes, both for investors like me and for uninsured Tennesseans. At Xantus's peak, we rated highest in customer satisfaction. I turned down an offer to sell the company, which I'd started on a $1 million personal loan, for $40 million. I dreamed of taking Xantus into the Fortune 500.

Soon, however, the road had turned rocky. The state began to renege on its contractual obligations, never paying promised rates to HMOs. Other HMO owners and I lost a good deal of money as we funded the state's shortfalls from our own pockets. Worse, judges were deciding in favor of patient advocates, forcing us to pay for treatments we'd never agreed to, and in essence, making business decisions for us. I was persevering, hoping that TennCare's bureaucratic mismanagement could be corrected. I'd even begun to talk to my board of directors about the prospect of suing the state to force correct accounting. I hoped it wouldn't come to that.

The honors and laudatory articles were welcome diversions from what I hoped would be temporary setbacks. Over the years, my fortune had risen and fallen so many times that I'd taken the phoenix, the mystical Egyptian bird that continually rose from its own ashes, as a personal symbol, and eventually named two companies for it. Most important, my faith and marriage had never been stronger; and my kids, Buddy and Anica, each with graduate business degrees from prestigious schools, had launched promising careers and showed every sign of outdoing me. I'd recruited my kids to help me start and run Xantus from its inception and they were still with me through these turbulent times. I couldn't have been prouder—or more grateful—for their help.

While thinking about all this on that particular Saturday morning, I unfolded the newspaper on the kitchen table while still standing . . . then froze. In the front-page photograph accompanying the Nashville *Tennessean*'s lead story, I was shocked to see my own features looking back at me. The huge headline was stacked three lines deep over the photo: "TBI PROBE OF XANTUS CONFIRMED."

Stunned, I scanned the article:

> The TBI confirmed an "open criminal investigation" by the bureau's Medicaid Fraud Control Unit . . . Spokesman Mark Gwyn wouldn't say when the probe began or characterize its extent . . . allegations from state regulators that Xantus Healthplan improperly transferred $10 million in state and federal funds to its parent company . . .

A court filing had questioned my judgment, accusing me personally of "mismanagement and breaches of fiduciary obligations."

Waves of anger, disgust, and hurt swept over me. Xantus and my name were interchangeable in Nashville. The transfer of funds between the companies had been completely proper—in fact, I'd plowed much more into the company than I'd ever taken out. But no one—*no one*—from the Tennessee Bureau of Investigation or any other law enforcement group had contacted me, my attorneys, or any Xantus representative with any questions whatsoever. In fact, they never would. (Almost a year after the story ran, I had my attorneys contact an assistant United States attorney to begin the process of clearing my name.)

I was devastated. I knew how hard it would be to overcome the crushing effects of these front-page accusations on my integrity. From the time I was a boy, I had protected the Howard name. Close friends and casual acquaintances know me as a straight arrow, solid in my faith and proud of my sterling reputation. I'd built a career "doing well by doing good," whether or not anyone was looking. Now I thought of my mother, who'd struggled so hard as a maid, and who endlessly repeated to her four children her favorite, paraphrased verse from Proverbs: "It is better to have a good name than all the riches in the world."

I called Karan, who was in Cleveland for a convention of The Links, Inc., an African American community service organization. She, too, was outraged and made attempts to comfort me.

Numb with shock, I went back into the bedroom after the phone call. Karan has always said she can tell when I'm down, because there's a sitting area in our bedroom that I gravitate to in times of trouble. From the edge of the couch I can see out the window, and I can see my mother's photograph on the table next to me. I spent the rest of the day alone at home, taking phone calls from sympathetic friends and family, wondering if everything I'd accomplished so far in my life would be destroyed.

I've scrupulously avoided injecting race into business matters during my entire career. But I couldn't help recalling a saying African Americans have repeated among themselves for generations: In the North you can get as high as you want, but don't get too close. In the South you can get as close as you want, but don't get too high.

I wondered about the timing of this investigation, having recently received all those honors. The interviews had certainly raised my profile as a successful entrepreneur. I wondered if it were a coincidence that African Americans headed two of Tennessee's three largest managed-care insurers, and, until recently, had posted record profits. The state would soon make similar accusations against Access MedPlus CEO Anthony Cebrun, also African American, eventually forcing his ouster.

I thought about the term "breach of fiduciary obligations." Did that mean that I was making too much money?

I reflected on my rise to success and on my personal symbol, the phoenix.

I had traveled a long way from the peanut fields of Marietta, Oklahoma, where I was born. That phoenix, the Egyptian emblem for redemption and regeneration, had become a metaphor for my own life: Everything I'd earned had come from nothing, and every deal I'd ever made had started from scratch. Every time I'd suffered a reversal of fortune, I'd come back even stronger.

Over the years, I'd suffered plenty of setbacks, including having a business go into bankruptcy. I'd emerged wiser, and eventually, wealthier than ever. I had learned long ago not to take criticism and hard luck personally.

This, however, was different. I threw myself into battle to save my company, my career, and my reputation.

As I write this, seven years after that fateful morning, Xantus is no more. After I voluntarily stepped down as CEO, which I hoped would save the company and many jobs, the court's appointed rehabilitators finally admitted what I'd said from the start: No one could make Xantus profitable when the state wasn't paying its share. Despite the rehabilitators' optimistic predictions, they couldn't find a buyer either—TennCare's inadequate funding had become common knowledge in the business community. The rehabilitators quietly shut down Xantus—but not before the state sued me for $9 million in allegedly lost or misused funds.

By the state's count, this failed "rehabilitation" cost over $12 million of legal, accounting, consulting, and rehabilitation fees, and over $47 million of claims overpayments to providers—for a total rehabilitation cost of more than $59 million. That $9 million I was falsely accused of taking starts to sound paltry in comparison, but I guess someone felt the losses needed to be explained somehow.

TennCare, too, is on life support; its projected increases now dwarfing the costs Medicaid incurred. After the governor announced his plan to kill the program and leave over four hundred thousand without coverage, a huge public outcry brought about a last-ditch effort to save TennCare. It may be too late for the concessions now on the table from patients' advocates, who know a return to Medicaid will be far worse for them.

Eventually, the federal government cleared me of wrongdoing and dropped their criminal investigation. After the front-page newspaper announcement of the investigation and years of costly litigation that I instigated to prove my innocence, the U.S. attorney for Middle Tennessee quietly issued a two-sentence letter to inform me they'd found nothing. The state's suit against me for $9 million was dropped, and my countersuit of $57 million of claims against the state was settled.

The last few years, starting with the moment I opened that newspaper, have been the worst of my life. Or perhaps I should say, I *hope* they're the worst.

When I first set out to write this book at the outset of this ordeal, I wanted to set the record straight about what I saw as a travesty of justice. I wanted to point out the bureaucratic blunders that thwarted much-needed help for our state's poor and sick—and potentially our nation's forty-four million uninsured. I wanted to include charts and references showing how the state underfunded TennCare, despite its contractual agreements. (And I still have them, if you're interested!) Because, you see, I think that the failures of petty individuals did more than destroy my company and its promise. They destroyed a great solution to one of our country's biggest problems.

Beyond the goal of correcting the record, I wanted most of all to encourage young people to pursue their entrepreneurial dreams. Yet, after all that's happened, some may wonder whether I'm the best example for young men and women to follow.

I've had time for a lot of soul-searching these last few years. And I finally came to terms with the fact that my own pride and hubris was part of my downfall. I'd worked hard all my life, in part because I wanted to stand on the shoulders of those who came before me, and to give a leg up to the next generation. The high profile I sought made me an attractive target.

I realized that my life still serves a larger purpose. I've lived through lots of tough times, including the loss of my biggest success. If you look at some of the most moving stories in the Bible concerning greatness and wisdom, you'll find travails. Nebuchadnezzar, who wandered about like a beast before returning to his former state of grace. Daniel in the lion's den. Shadrach, Meshach, and Abednego, seen in a fiery furnace, dancing and singing, ready for the next life.

Their stories are much like that of the phoenix—that which is no longer useful gives way to something new.

So I abandoned my original idea and headed in another direction. As my wife has often pleaded, I'm going to stop "helping God."

This book is not about settling scores. It's about overcoming, and thriving, especially for people of color, for women, for the handicapped, the disadvantaged, and the young—but ultimately, it's for anyone who wants to succeed. I've made my way without playing the race card or depending on affirmative action. I believe affirmative action is limiting. If I can make it and overcome my obstacles, so can you.

Despite everything that's happened, I remain convinced that America's free enterprise system is the best in the world. I want to let young people know that, whatever their backgrounds, America's field of dreams offers level play. I want to help prepare individuals to live a better life. Success isn't just about prosperity. Becoming a better businessman has also meant becoming a better father, husband, brother, son, and citizen. Reaping spiritual and material rewards has meant living life to the fullest, savoring its sweetness and blessings, and surviving its hardships. On all those subjects, I have a bird's-eye view.

CHAPTER 1

GOING HOME

Therefore put on the full armor of God, so that when the day of evil comes, you may be able to stand your ground, and after you have done everything, to stand.

—Ephesians 6:13 (NIV)

Sometimes a crisis helps you focus on what's important. If you pay attention, you'll find God's messages everywhere, guiding you through your toughest struggles. That's what happened shortly after that story in the *Tennessean* appeared.

I guess I've always been something of a do-gooder. When I was growing up, I was so serious about my goals that no one dared make fun of me. (Or if they did, I was so focused that I didn't notice.) After I became an adult, I always played by the rules. My wife still reminds me about the time I drove miles out of our way to return ten dollars to a Kmart because the cashier gave us too much change. I hadn't noticed until we were long gone, but I insisted on returning it. The cashier might never have noticed, but I would have.

Still, there's a difference between being a do-gooder and a goody-two-shoes. I have never backed down from a battle. I wanted with every fiber of my being to defeat my adversaries and regain my standing in the community.

13

After the *Tennessean*'s story ran, I began to find out who my real friends were. Even before the news of the criminal investigation hit the papers, many had stepped forward to publicly question the motives of the state rehabilitators and to support me personally. Others wrote letters to the editor of the *Tennessean*, attesting to my good character. Former mentors Jack Anderson of Hospital Affiliates and HCA CEO Thomas Frist went on the record on my behalf, unwavering in their support. Many more wrote or called me to boost my spirits. Their words meant more than I can say.

Along with my business associates and friends, the *Tennessean*'s story about the TBI investigation into Xantus galvanized the African American community. The *Urban Journal*, Nashville's African American paper, ran an interview allowing me to give my side of the story. A group of prominent black leaders, many of them ministers, called on Governor Don Sundquist to ask that I be treated fairly. "We're disappointed with this state and with the governor," said one. For many—including me—the issue boiled down to integrity. State Senator Thelma Harper said she believed the investigation was racially motivated. "They think he got too big," she told the *Tennessean*.

I've always been a strong believer in prayer; it changes the environment. And I was doing a lot of praying those days. I also believe that God speaks as well as listens. We just have to keep our ears open. For me, the messages often come between the hours of two and four in the morning. When I wake up, I know what God wants me to do.

Apparently God also speaks to others in the same way. During a visit to Kansas City to visit family and friends during the Fourth of July, just a few days after the story ran, we took Karan's brother out for a good steak dinner to celebrate his sixty-first birthday. Marvin and I go back a long way, even further than his sister, Karan, and I. He just seems to pop up at turning points in my life.

We enjoyed each other's company, as we always do. Marvin read the newspaper accounts I had brought for him to see, but he didn't seem to have much to say about what had happened in Nashville.

After he went to bed that night, the news of my problems must have gone to work on him. Marvin told us later that he woke up suddenly at 3:00 A.M. and knew he had to immediately call a good friend who was also a criminal attorney. He shared the articles with his friend and asked him to meet with us at my friend's home before we returned to Nashville. I guess criminal attorneys are used to getting calls at 3:00 A.M., because he came to Gary Ballard's home the next morning.

Until that meeting, I had been convinced that, because I had done nothing wrong, I couldn't be indicted. Attorney Joe Johnson took the *Tennessean* clipping and underlined the words "breach of fiduciary obligations." He explained that the term was so broad that a U.S. attorney could use it to mean almost anything. In fact, he said, a U.S. attorney could use it "to indict a ham sandwich." Johnson warned me that because of my prominence and visibility, I was a perfect target for an aggressive assistant U.S. attorney who was looking to build his reputation.

Johnson recommended good criminal attorneys in Knoxville, whom he suggested I meet with as soon as possible after I returned to Tennessee. He said he would call them that night. The lawyers contacted me immediately upon my return to Nashville and instructed me to bring a box of material to Knoxville as soon as possible. I complied, and they were very helpful in educating me about the challenges ahead. The attorneys were also Christians. One of them later resigned to become a priest.

At that first meeting, however, slowly, surely, as he spoke, I began to understand. The destruction of my good name was only the beginning. If my adversaries won this battle, I could go to jail.

In a way, Marvin's 3:00 A.M. wake-up call to that attorney was also my own. Through it all, my wife and family were solidly behind me. Karan told me, "No matter what happens, Sam, God has something better for you on the other side of this." *But what would that be?*

Only a couple of weeks after news of the criminal investigation hit the papers, Karan and I traveled back to Lawton, Oklahoma, where I grew up. I'd already started work on this book, and I wanted to refresh my memories of the people and places that had shaped me.

Even when I was very young, I always had a job. Lawton gave me my first business experience, whether it was delivering papers or working in a grocery store or a meat-packing plant. We didn't have much at home, but I always had some kind of dream: to be a professional musician; to be president; to be *somebody*, as Dr. Martin Luther King Jr. would later say, and to accomplish great things. My mother, who worked as a maid, and my father, who worked in a tire shop, helped me the best way they knew how—by setting good examples. They worked hard and honestly, and they loved and protected their children. Their actions spoke louder than any words.

Life in Lawton came back to me in a rush.

I drove past the abandoned grocery store where I once worked, and the sign outside was unreadable. The meat-packing plant at which I had worked was half tumbled down, and now a vacant lot stood where my family's first house had been. The old school, Douglass High, was where my sixth-grade teacher, Mr. Albert Johnson, had paddled me because someone informed him I'd crossed the railroad tracks in front of an oncoming train.

While in Lawton, I spoke with Mr. Johnson and others who had known me as a youngster. Mr. Johnson is retired but still active in educating Lawton's schoolchildren. (He told me he had stopped spanking kids years earlier.)

I visited my brother Maurice, who lives outside Oklahoma City. I also visited my sister Callie, and she prepared some fried chicken from Mother's recipe using Swans flour. Callie still lives in our family's second house, the place we all remember as home. It's just a small house—with three bedrooms and one big living/dining area—by today's standards, a tiny place for six people. Callie keeps the place spotless, and much of Mom and Dad's original furniture is still there. Our parents' bedroom is exactly as it was when they lived there, with the old heavy furniture, chenille bedspread, and plywood knickknack shelf I made in shop class. In some ways it is almost like a shrine. Callie says she often feels our parents' presence there, and it's a comfort to her.

Callie and her daughter, Gail, sing in the choir at Bethlehem Baptist Church, and Gail's husband, Michael, is a minister there, as well as a song leader and soloist. The four children in our family had all attended Bethlehem Baptist Church, just down the block from our first home. I was baptized there when I was twelve. Mother attended another church. (Daddy, who worked many days from 4:00 A.M. to 10:30 P.M., wasn't much of a churchgoer.) Bethlehem Baptist Church had since moved to a new location, in a big, modern building.

Karan and I attended the Sunday morning service during our stay in Lawton. During the church service, I felt the hand of God tapping on my shoulder again. In the parking lot, on our way into the church, I had just told Karan, "In the next speech I give, I want to talk about Romans 8:28." I didn't know that would be in the next few minutes!

From the moment I walked in the door, Bethlehem welcomed me like a long-lost son. As the service started, the organ, piano, bass, guitar, and drums, along with the large choir and featured soloists, swung into the music. They sang familiar old hymns and contemporary Christian music. In one of the opening numbers, the choir rocked through "Long As I Got King Jesus," a James Cleveland hymn, following a spirited soloist in classic call-and-response style:

I been lied on
Lied on!
Cheated
Cheated!
Talked about
Mistreated
Oooooo

I been 'buked
'Buked!
Scorned
Scorned!
Talked about, sure as I'm born

I been up
Up!
Down
Down!
Almost to the ground

But long as I got King Jesus
I don't need nobody else . . .

It felt as if every word in that service were meant for me. Or as Callie put it later, "The minister was all in Sam's face today."

A young man came forward to say that his unit had recently been deployed to Kuwait, and he would soon go overseas. The pastor quoted a verse that had long been close to my heart: "No weapon that is formed against thee shall prosper." The rest of that passage continues ". . . and every tongue that shall rise against thee in judgment thou shalt condemn. This is the heritage of the servants of the Lord." It had always been one of my favorite passages. "God is going to make a way," said the minister.

I had never met Pastor Gary Bender before, but he called my name to come forward and say a few words to the congregation.

I've spoken to many gatherings, and I've been told I give a pretty good speech, but this was different somehow. I was even a little nervous. I've never been afraid to talk about my faith and discuss Scripture, but I had never before given Christian testimony in a church.

I walked to the podium and looked out at the crowd, all smiling expectantly. To them, I was the hometown kid who'd made good. It would be hard to explain that not everything was going well. But I needed their help.

After thanking the congregation for its warm welcome, I explained what was happening.

> I'm facing a lot of challenges. The state of Tennessee is investigating my corporation. But I've done no wrong. I ask for your prayers. Scripture says, in Romans 8:28, "And we know that in all things God works together for the good of those who love him, who have been called according to his purpose." That's what I'm counting on.

Many in the congregation got up to shake my hand or embrace me as I walked, deeply moved, from the front of the church back to my seat. Karan's eyes were filled with tears.

The pastor's sermon that day was about the story of Hagar and her young son, who were dying of thirst in the desert. Hagar left the child so she wouldn't have to see him die. Then God "opened her eyes" to a well of water and both were saved. "You'll find God's help in unexpected places," said Reverend Bender. "Sometimes you just have to stop trying to help him."

Karan and I touched hands at this and smiled. She had often said that I worked too hard trying to help God, when I needed to sit back and let Him tell me what He wanted me to do. Sitting back is hard to do if you're used to being in charge of a big company with a lot of employees who are counting on you. But I began to understand that this must be what God wanted me to do.

The service closed with a slow, poignant version of a hymn that's been my favorite for many years: "On Christ the Solid Rock I Stand."

I realized later that the church service was sort of a second baptism. It felt like a baptism by fire, and I knew a phoenix would rise again from the ashes. I just had to wait and see where God wanted me to fly.

A feeling of peace fell over me. In the coming weeks, I made the most painful business decision of my career: I would step down from Xantus. I wouldn't, however, accept a condition of immunity from criminal prosecution. I would demand the opportunity to clear my name.

I trusted God to guide me through this crisis. Wherever He led me, I would follow. I would do all I could, and stand.

CHAPTER 2

As the Twig Is Bent, So Grows the Tree

Train up a child in the way he should go,
and when he is old he will not depart from it.

—Proverbs 22:6 (NKJV)

My parents, Nellie and Houston Howard, grew up on peanut farms near Marietta, Oklahoma, not far from the Red River and the Texas border. Their parents worked very hard for little money, but at least they owned their land. Their people were proud and independent, or as proud and independent as African Americans could be in Oklahoma in the years after the Dust Bowl and Depression.

My mother's folks died when she was young, so I didn't get to know them. But we kids would spend summers with my father's parents, Molly and Beda Howard, on their peanut farm. I'd work all summer, chopping peanuts for ten cents a row, and staying thin because the work was hard. They had a lot of land.

I'm not sure how or why the Howards settled in Oklahoma. It may have had something to do with the Homestead Act of 1860, which offered free land to U.S. citizens who were willing to settle in the West. There were several all-black towns in the West after the Civil War, populated by those who had fled the oppressive South. That western sense of independence is, I believe, a critical feature of African American progress. Even today, I can detect that self-determination in descendants of black westerners who resettled in the South years ago.

African Americans weren't immune from problems in Oklahoma. Although they weren't far away, because of their isolated lives on farms in the southern part of the state, I'm almost positive that my parents and grandparents never heard about the Tulsa race riot of 1921, which cost hundreds or perhaps thousands of African American lives. It began with a newspaper's false account of rape after a black man touched a white woman's arm. The riot wore on for hours. Survivors today recount seeing incendiary devices dropped from the air, which helped to destroy the vibrant black commercial district of Greenwood, also known as the Black Wall Street. The story was so unreported or minimized in white newspapers of the day that historians are still trying to determine how many were killed and how many were buried in mass graves.

Miles from that scene of urban violence, the Howards quietly persevered on their farms, instilled with a work ethic that survives in my own children today.

Dad wanted to be a pitcher in the Negro Leagues, but his dream ended when he injured his arm. After my parents got married, they moved from Marietta, where I was born in 1939, to Lawton, Oklahoma, and took jobs. Lawton, about 100 miles southwest of Oklahoma City, is by no means a big city. But the military base, Fort Sill, fueled a bustling commercial district there—one of the biggest in the region. Today about eighty thousand people live in Lawton. I'd guess it was half that size when I moved there. I was about six, the oldest of four children. Lula was a couple of years younger, followed by Maurice and Callie.

During the worst days of the Depression, people lived in shanties and tepees along Lawton's dirt roads. But World War II and its aftermath brought prosperity to the military town. At first we rented a house on Arlington Street. Just about all I remember of the place are the hardwood floors and the fruit trees across the street. Callie remembers that we kids all learned Pig Latin there. Later, Mother and Dad bought the house on Carver Street that Callie still lives in today.

In a way, my parents first exposed me to the business world and professionals by moving from the farm. Like most Oklahoma towns in the 1940s, Lawton was segregated. One found our part of Lawton where one would find most small-town black communities—across the railroad tracks.

Through the years, the railroad tracks that so often divide black and white sections of town became another sort of personal symbol for me. Like the phoenix, railroads represent migration and metamorphosis, progress from one state to another. I have some beautiful pieces of art today that capture that sentiment—African American artists like John Biggers and Jacob Lawrence realized the powerful significance of trains and tracks for black people. As artist Romare Bearden once said, "I use the train as a symbol of the other civilization and its encroachment upon the lives of blacks. The train was always something that could take you away and could also bring you where you were. And in the little towns it's the black people who live near the trains."

Despite their divisive nature, railroads represented the Industrial Revolution, which created jobs available to newly freed slaves. In turn, railroads also spawned those early African American business-world heroes, the Pullman porters. In the 1930s, the sleeping car porters, many of them college educated, formed the first black union in the United States, pulling together to create better lives and wages for themselves and their families. They didn't earn much from George Pullman, but their tips often exceeded their salaries. They worked hard but lived in nice homes and enjoyed literature and music.

They probably made more money than anybody else except black baseball players or funeral directors.

Aside from helping to create the first self-sufficient black middle class, Pullman porters served as a sort of CNN for blacks across the country as they delivered African American newspapers such as the Atlanta *Daily World*, the Pittsburgh *Courier*, and the Chicago *Defender* to small towns along their route. Their union was also one of the first black professional organizations to help effect positive social change, helping to underwrite the civil rights movement. Later, a Pullman dining car would be the site of a significant turning point in my own career.

Bound for Freedom

In the 1930s, railroad sleeping car porters' jobs had become one of the most desirable for blacks. In the '40s, led by A. Phillip Randolph, the group unionized and won pay increases and other rights, such as shedding the derisive name "George" for every Pullman porter (from George Pullman). By the 1950s, the Pullman porters lived well, and their contributions were critical to Dr. Martin Luther King Jr.'s successful protests in the deep South.

In 1955, the Pullman porters agreed they would donate two dollars of their pay each week to the National Association for the Advancement of Colored People (NAACP)—a nice piece of money back then, because many only made five dollars a week.

One Pullman porter, Edgar D. Nixon, became president of the NAACP in Montgomery, Alabama. He asked the most articulate young guy in town to be spokesman for the Montgomery Improvement Association. So Martin Luther King Jr. became the spokesman for the MIA. Nixon and the others had been looking for an opportunity to protest Montgomery's segregated buses. It was the elite class of blacks who were hurt and embarrassed by the Jim Crow laws. They would get on the bus with their nice suits and ties and have to sit at the back.

Nixon's secretary at the local NAACP was Rosa Parks. She had been working with him in the NAACP since 1944. They planned her nonviolent act of noncooperation—refusing to give up her seat in the front of the bus to a white. When Parks went to jail for it, the NAACP launched its boycott. Nixon and the others used the money from the Pullman porters to arrange for station wagons and private cars to take people to work. The boycott was successful, and the buses were integrated.

A. Phillip Randolph, who had forced George Pullman to the bargaining table with the porters, organized the 1963 March on Washington. He said the best way to put it together was to let the NAACP have the lead and then call other groups in. So they called in the whole coalition—King's group, the Southern Christian Leadership Conference (SCLC), Whitney Young, the Urban League, John Lewis, and the Student Nonviolent Coordinating Committee (SNCC).

There were twenty-four speakers that day, and King was last on the list. By the time he got to the podium, it was late afternoon. After all, the SCLC was young, and King was a newcomer to the organization who had only been on the scene five or six years. Yet, of all the speeches that were made that day, King's is the one people remember. Nobody remembers what A. Phillip Randolph, Roy White, or Roy Wilkins said; all that's remembered is the "I have a dream" speech.

—Dr. Bobby Lovett, history professor, Tennessee State University; author of works including A Black Man's Dream: First 100 Years and The African American History of Nashville, 1780–1930

Like many segregated black communities, our neighborhood in Lawton was small. A few blocks housed every socioeconomic level: teachers, ministers, the black doctor, the black dentist, morticians, and store owners lived next door to janitors, factory workers, and taxi drivers.

Today, however, in addition to the railroad tracks, giant pillars holding up Interstate 44 cross the neighborhood. Some of the black community still lives in those small, wood-frame houses. A few have fallen into disrepair, but many are well-maintained and have been renovated and expanded. Expensive cars are parked in a few driveways. Successful African American professionals no longer have to live in this neighborhood, but many still choose to do so.

Lawton doesn't look that much different today from the way it did when I grew up there. I wonder, though, whether the black community could be as tightly knit as it was back then.

Long before today's working couples struggled to cope with raising families, our community pulled together to bring up their children. Not many African American wives could afford to be stay-at-home moms. Their husbands struggled to scratch out a living in the few jobs available to them, and the wives helped out the best they could. In our neighborhood, the parents supported each other. Every adult in the area served as a substitute parent for any child within shouting distance. You were just as likely to be spanked by a neighbor's father as your own, if he happened to be the one who witnessed your crime.

We children were raised to respect every elder, black or white. We always used "Mr." or "Mrs." and said, "Yes, sir," and "No, ma'am." When whites called our fathers "boy" and our mothers by their first names, we just thought they must not have been raised right. During a recent conversation, my brother reminded me of something. Despite his difficult life, Dad never talked about racism. We all knew it existed, but he never taught us to hate white people.

One of the few things I remember about Nanny (our name for Dad's mother), was how quiet she was. Dad was like her in that respect. In his few hours off work, he would just sit, silently presiding over a room. He didn't say much, but his presence was reassuring. Dad's countless hours of work and sacrifice for the family taught me the power of deeds over words. He was my first mentor.

I must have inherited my ability to work hard and long from my father, who took a job at Montgomery Ward mounting tires. In time he was promoted to manager, but that was as far as he got. He accepted that he wouldn't be permitted to rise any higher there, so he took on one or sometimes two other jobs. He'd get up at four o'clock in the morning and go wash windows. Then he'd come home and make breakfast: rice and eggs, fried hard. He'd pack a bologna sandwich for lunch and go back to work. After he finished a full day at Montgomery Ward, he'd go to Fort Sill and wash dishes until about ten-thirty each evening.

My father was there to provide for us. He worked for Montgomery Ward for twenty-five years. When he retired, the company gave him a watch. I still have it, and it will go to my son someday.

Although she worked outside our home as a maid, my mother's most important jobs were to love us, feed us, and clothe us. She was the center of our family. She must have been tired a lot, but we all remember her praying out loud or singing hymns praising God as she worked around the house. Sometimes she would have her friends over. Many of them were also maids, and they'd sit at the dining room table, drinking coffee and talking and laughing.

Both of my parents took pride in their jobs and did them to the best of their ability. My father could mount a tire in the blink of an eye. My mother's employers gave her keys to their homes. I can't remember either of them ever calling in sick.

I knew from an early age that my parents worked hard, but I didn't know that a lot of people thought of us as poor. My two sisters and brother and I had plenty to eat, good clothes, a nice house, and presents at Christmas and birthdays. My mother dressed the two girls alike. When Lula was elected homecoming queen in her senior year in high school, money was found to buy her a gown.

We felt loved and protected. We always knew exactly where our boundaries were and what the consequences would be if we crossed them. Like most kids, we felt safer knowing those boundaries were there, even as we tested them. My mother was the disciplinarian, and back then no one considered spankings to be beatings. With all our parents' rules, however, we never felt constrained.

My big rebellion came when I was thirteen—I decided I would never wear jeans again, choosing dress slacks instead. I had begun to buy my own clothes as soon as I started earning paychecks. I guess I always liked nice threads!

Everyone wore their very finest clothes on Sunday. The ushers at Bethlehem Baptist wore somber black suits and white gloves, and followed carefully established rules of order. Becoming a deacon involved a rigorous series of duties and responsibilities, something I discovered firsthand when I became one in my Nashville church.

No matter how old we got, Mother always got us up to go to church. "If you can go out on Saturday night, you can go to church on Sunday," she'd say. We kids walked to Sunday school and church, where we could visit with our friends. It was the center of our spiritual lives, and the Reverend O. B. Davis baptized all four of us. My brother and sisters are all still active churchgoers and devoutly religious. My brother Maurice sells insurance and works with computers. But I believe he has a special calling to the ministry, and I hope he will one day enter a seminary for formal study.

Like many black churches, Bethlehem Baptist did more than preach to the converted. Anyone who's been a member of a strong African American church knows what a positive force it can be. It's no wonder that black churches were such an important part of the civil rights movement. Bethlehem Baptist was one of the seams that bound our community together. In addition to helping see that its members were fed and clothed and sheltered, the church provided order and spiritual solace.

The biblical lessons I learned in church helped me understand what made a good man and why I wanted to be one. My siblings and I found black mentors and role models there, from the preacher and deacons, to the ushers and members of the choir and auxiliary.

Every Sunday after church we'd go back home to fried chicken, mashed potatoes, green beans, corn bread, banana cake, fried apricot pies—the works. Mother made the best fried chicken I ever ate, and it was always made with Swans flour and Crisco.

I started a paper route when I was eight so I could buy a sharp Schwinn bike, with mud flaps and shock-absorbing springs. I was *bad* on that bike.

When I got a little older, I took a job at Mrs. Octavia Johnson's store, People's Grocery, on Dearborn Street. That's where my business education began. I swept the floor, stocked shelves, bagged groceries, did whatever needed doing—all for the grand sum of eight dollars a week. I had to learn to be on time every day, and I watched and learned as Mrs. Johnson dealt with customers and suppliers. She also told me how to dress neatly for work and gave me other useful tips. In those days, our teachers—those who taught inside the school building as well as those who taught about real life outside of it—took responsibility for their students.

We had some remarkable teachers inside the school. I will always remember our principal, Mr. Sadberry, walking the hall, telling us, "Satisfied! Never be satisfied!" Miss Patterson was a great math teacher, and it was she who got me interested in numbers. Eagle-eyed Albert Johnson roamed the hallways—even today, I wouldn't dream of addressing him as anything but "Mr. Johnson." When he became principal, he saw to it that the grounds were always neat and clean, and that assemblies were quiet and orderly. We knew we might have to mop the hallway if we were late to school. Another principal, Mr. Shegog, would ask us, "Did you go to church on Sunday?" It was like family. Every teacher pushed us to do something.

When I turned seventeen, I took a job stuffing sausages at a local meat-packing plant, Lawton Meat Supply. After my father, the owner, Marlin Keathley, was the next-important mentor to me. When it was time to enter college, he cosigned a loan for me. Every summer I worked full-time at the meat-packing plant to pay off the loan. Mr. Keathley gave me five dollars each week and put the rest in the bank. I arrived at work every morning at six o'clock, after walking the mile and a half from home. Later I earned fellowships and didn't have to continue borrowing so heavily, but that's how I made it to college. Marlin Keathley made sure I was able to go.

I still have the tax receipt for the first summer I worked at the plant. I earned $676.10 during three months in 1957.

I was so serious, so focused, and had so few girlfriends that my high school classmates had a little fun with my senior photo and listing in the yearbook. There, I was listed as: "Most Likely to Succeed. Three-time governor of the state of Oklahoma. Leader of new progressive party. His motto: All for one, and that one me. Candidate for presidency last year—defeated by one vote, cast by his campaign manager. Unmarried."

High Expectations

Sam was always a serious student. The school had a reputation based on those who went before. And his mother
had high expectations of her children. I carried a wooden
paddle back then—and I knew where everyone was at 9:30.
I've learned since that there are other ways of dealing with
discipline. But if you show children you care, they will do
what you ask. I was a taskmaster, but they respected me.

—Albert Johnson, former principal,
Douglass High, Lawton, Oklahoma

He would see planes in the sky, and he used to tell our
father, "Daddy, I'm going to fly those jets." He would
say, "I want to be president one day." When he told Karan's
mother that, she said, "If it's going to be anyone black, it will
be you." That's the thing about Sam. He knows he is in
charge of his own destiny.

All I've ever known is "how well your brother did this or
that." But it was like a carpet ride, a favor. It was a ticket to
a little special treatment. It gave us all some goals. That's
what Sam was to all of us.

—Maurice Howard, brother,
Midwest City, Oklahoma

Lots of things were different in those days, some better
and some worse. We said the Pledge of Allegiance every day,
and the principal led us in the Lord's Prayer. I believe that
those simple rituals helped shape us all in a positive way.
What good does it do you to learn all the science and history
in the world, if you don't have a personal moral compass to
help guide your actions? It's no wonder so many of our

young people are so directionless. That kind of guidance is crucial today, when the schools are full of children from so many different backgrounds. I believe if you pray together, you don't kill each other.

Back then the schools were segregated. Without question, the end of forced separation of the races, ruled inherently unequal by the Supreme Court in 1954, was a long-awaited step forward for African Americans and for our society as a whole. In 1960, I wrote a speech called "If There Were a Law," which was later published in a book compiled by the Interstate Oratorical Association. Four years before the Civil Rights Act mandated an end to forced segregation in public places, I unequivocally took my stand:

> Segregation has inflicted a wound upon the soul of the segregated and so restricted his mind that some have come to believe that it is useless to strive for the highest and the best . . . Restricting the full development of a group in a nation retards its own growth and development. The minority produces less, and the superior group spends too much time seeking ways and means of keeping the minority in "its place" because they are afraid to pursue the whole truth. Segregating the Negro leads to injustice, brutality, and lynching by the majority. As a rule, equal justice in the courts is almost impossible for a member of the Negro group if it involves a member of the group imposing segregation . . .

> The time to begin is now. The place to begin is within your minds . . .

> The world is now too small for reaction and prejudice. What we do among ourselves has repercussions for the rest of the world. Those of you who are white are having, and so far wasting, your last chance to be accepted on an equal basis with the other peoples of a world that is two-thirds colored. The 300-year advantage you have had through the Industrial Revolution is coming to a close as the remainder of the world becomes industrialized . . .

Integration meant that at last public places would be open to everyone. No longer would the black population of Lawton have to go down an alley and climb a flight of stairs to the balcony of the Ritz Theater to watch a movie through a pane of glass. No longer would our evenings out and dinners be restricted to "our places," like Johnny's Barbecue or Calvin's, a nightspot with a dirt floor. No longer would our children's school facilities, books, and programs be separate and markedly inferior to those of the whites.

But with these gains, our community paradoxically suffered a loss. The law meant Douglass High would be closed, and many of our beloved black teachers and school administrators would lose their jobs or be relegated to lower positions. Going to an all-black school meant that all our role models and mentors were accomplished men and women of color, which we students could easily envision ourselves becoming. It was invaluable to observe these role models every day so we could pattern ourselves after them. Many people credit an admired teacher with helping them find their paths in life.

Like their black students, the black faculty and administrators who kept their jobs became minorities among a sea of whites. Black children were no longer surrounded by black adults they could look up to.

Going to an all-black school offered other advantages. For example, my wife, Karan, loved acting in plays, but she went to an integrated high school, which meant she could not audition for leading roles. The only parts available to her were those of servants.

A history of Lawton's Douglass High described the day the students received news the school would be closed to comply with *Brown v. Board of Education, Topeka, Kansas*: "On that day, the Lion wept" (the school's mascot was a lion). By the year it closed, the school had graduated both a National Merit scholar and a White House fellow.

Today I often advise young African Americans to go to a historically black college for their undergraduate education. It's a good way to explore all your possibilities without any limitations and to get yourself anchored in your own identity at the same time. After that, go to the best graduate school you can find in your field. My son and daughter went to Morehouse and Spelman Colleges, both in Atlanta, before going on to earn additional undergraduate and graduate degrees at Georgia Tech, Duke, and Vanderbilt. Karan and I recently sent our godson on a tour of historically black colleges. I told him he could go anywhere he wanted, but I was sending his check to Morehouse.

Despite my very small universe, bounded by the railroad tracks and the street that divided the white community from the black in Lawton, Oklahoma, I never felt limited. I was secure at home. I dreamed big, and everyone encouraged me. I did so well at school that my teachers often said they knew I would make something of myself.

I was such a serious student that some people were surprised that I had a girlfriend. We went to football games, to the ice cream shop, and in those last days of segregation, to Johnny's, or Calvin's. Of course, we also saw each other at school every day.

But after I went to college, she began seeing others. Eventually I heard that she'd become pregnant. I was sad and so disappointed in her. She must not have understood that she had choices, and she must not have understood the path she'd chosen to walk as an unwed mother.

So many people don't understand what a privilege and responsibility children are. Everyone has choices, and men and women should remember that having a child too young, especially outside of marriage, can severely limit their own development, as well as that of their children's. Children need a mother and a father and a stable home life, and it's hard to find that kind of home and relationship outside of marriage. Too often it falls to the women to define what a relationship will or won't be. Men, especially African American men, must also take responsibility for making choices about sex and child-rearing.

Don't get me wrong. Most of my beliefs fit into the conservative mold, but I also firmly believe in personal freedom of choice. I don't think the government should be involved in prosecuting victimless crimes between consenting adults. What people do in their own bedrooms is their own business.

But bringing children into a relationship changes the equation in many ways. A child will change the parents economically, emotionally, and physically. And if they are doing their job right, those parents positively will influence that child.

As the twig is bent, so grows the tree. I am thankful for that truth in my life, for I couldn't have asked for stronger oaks than my own parents.

CHAPTER 3

EARLY YEARS

For we walk by faith, not by sight.

—2 Corinthians 5:7 (NKJV)

I believe my life and career have progressed because of divine providence. There's no way that chance could have dealt the opportunities that came my way at just the right moments. So many times, God has sent the right people to me at the right time, and thank heavens, I had enough sense—most of the time—to listen to them. As the saying goes, "Show me a self-made man and I'll show you poor workmanship."

My father and Marlin Keathley were the first two, and most important, influences in my growing-up years. But one piece of critical advice came from my high school band director, Levi Presley. In high school I dreamed of doing a lot of different things, and one of my first serious ambitions was to be a musician because I was a pretty good saxophone player.

Mr. Presley probably saved me many years of struggle by advising me to find something else. I was a decent-enough clarinet and saxophone player, and I eventually became student band director. But Mr. Presley knew I needed to do something other than music. Without his advice, I would probably have become just another fairly good musician competing against many thousands of others. If Levi Presley hadn't encouraged me to go to college, I probably wouldn't have given the idea much thought.

I cannot remember what force directed me to Oklahoma State University, a predominantly white college in Stillwater, but I found myself standing in front of the college of business one day. I can't even remember why I was in the area, but without much thought I decided to go inside and register. I had only $240 to my name. Fortunately, the tuition in 1957 was only $80.

A man in the registrar's office watched while I filled out the forms. He told me, "You're going to be the only black registered in OSU's college of business. Frankly, there probably won't be a job for you when you graduate."

The business world then was still an exclusive white fraternity. There was no such thing as affirmative action and no scholarship programs for minorities. My best hope, the man said, was to earn a PhD and teach because "the world is not ready for a black business executive."

Langston University, a black school, was only twenty-five miles away, but I decided to stay at OSU and focus on getting myself ready for any opportunities that might come my way. I couldn't change the whole world; I could only prepare myself. I still believe that if you concentrate on what you can do, God will take care of everything else.

My first year at OSU is a good example. After I enrolled, God steered another important counselor my way. Dr. Eugene Swearingen, dean of OSU's business school, for some reason took note of me in my first year of school. He must have liked what he saw because he offered to ease my financial burden by letting me teach a class. In my sophomore year, I began teaching a statistics lab two nights a week. That covered my tuition and went a little way toward room and board.

I thought about quitting school after my sophomore year. Money was very tight, and I wondered whether I should just go out and find a job. I was fortunate that my father, who spoke only when it was important, said, "Don't worry about the money. You should keep going to school." So, of course, I went back. I knew Dad was behind me.

At times I felt out of place. I'd grown up eating buttermilk and corn bread as a meal. I'd never felt ashamed of my background, but one evening, at a banquet, I noticed I was the only person in the room eating fried chicken with my fingers. That experience was unpleasant enough to prompt me to take an OSU course on etiquette during my senior year. I learned to eat chicken with a knife and fork, and I've never eaten it with my hands since—just as I never wore jeans after switching to dress slacks. My wife and I made sure we taught etiquette to our children, so they would also feel at home in any circumstance.

I did well in school, and I took some graduate courses after finishing in 1961. During the summers of 1961 and '62, I took a job with the United States Commerce Department in Washington, D.C. That first exposure to how government and big business works was an invaluable experience, but like a lot of entry-level jobs, it left me flat broke.

One day in Washington, as I was getting my hair cut at my uncle's barbershop, I met a young Howard University medical student named Marvin Wilson. We became fast friends, and we still are. As I mentioned earlier, Marvin seems to pop up and play important roles at critical moments in my life.

As summer drew to a close, I wondered how I would manage to get back home for a visit before going back to school. Marvin mentioned he would be driving home to Ottawa, Kansas, and he suggested I ride with him to his house, then catch a bus to Lawton. He had a little car that used more oil than gas, but I didn't have a car at all. I took him up on his suggestion.

We arrived in Ottawa on Friday of Labor Day weekend. That's when I met his sister, Karan. She was in school then, putting herself through Emporia State to earn her bachelor's degree in teaching. We hit it off immediately, and I kept putting off my departure. Sure, she was pretty and smart, but more important, she had a warm, wonderful personality that simply made me want to be with her. Within a couple of days we were inseparable, and that week I asked her to marry me. I never did make it home to Lawton during that trip; I left from Ottawa to go directly back to school in Stillwater.

Karan changed my life, for the better, in so many ways. We were of one mind and heart, but she also complemented me, made me complete. Before I met her, I was a loner. She was always drawn to people and gatherings—she fit in easily in any situation. In later years, she effortlessly adapted to the

A Whirlwind Romance

I grew up in Ottawa, Kansas, the youngest of four children, with three brothers. So you can imagine how protected I was. I'd be sitting on the front porch, and someone would come by and my dad would say, "Sorry, guys, Karan isn't permitted to have male guests visit, so you'll have to go somewhere else." Still, I had admirers and eventually my father let me date my senior year of high school.

The town had about ten thousand people, but less than one hundred were black. My family was close-knit, lots of fun. Dad worked for a furniture store and installed floor coverings for them. Mom worked part of the time for a laundry and dry cleaning company. At other times she did others' laundry and ironing at home. I guess you would have considered us to be lower middle-class. Neither parent completed high school, but it was Dad's dream that all four children would be college graduates. When he spoke to me, it was never "after you finish high school," it was always "after you finish college."

I was living at home for the summer between my junior and senior years at Emporia State when I met Sam. My brother Marvin wrote to me saying he was bringing a guy home to visit with him from Washington, D.C., and that he would appreciate my saving some time to help entertain him. We accommodated each other in that way. According to Sam, it was his intention to catch the bus to Lawton in Kansas City and spend the week with his family before returning to Oklahoma State. Marvin persuaded Sam to catch the bus from Ottawa rather than in Kansas City, so he could get a good meal and perhaps save money on the fare.

There was a strong attraction from the start.

As with most holidays, the house was filled with my relatives from neighboring towns. There was a family poker game going on as well as pokeno. Sam chose the family poker game against my warnings and it wasn't long till he lost his money. I rescued him by encouraging him to play pokeno for pennies with me. By Monday everyone began to notice our attraction to one another because we were inseparable. Before Sam left on the very last bus he could take on Thursday night in order to get to OSU by Friday morning for a scheduled meeting, he had asked me to marry him (that was five days after we met). I said I would marry him, but wasn't sure he was serious—until Christmas, when he gave me a diamond engagement ring and asked again if I would marry him. This time there was no question in my mind as to how he felt about me or how much I loved him.

I truly believe that God had His hand in our meeting and our union.

—Karan Howard

highest levels of Nashville society—and they to her. She always appears to be enjoying herself, at ease and confident in so many photos of charity balls or benefits, where we stand out, in full evening dress, as the only African Americans in a sea of white faces. Today, that ratio is beginning to change. I've always considered Nashville an open and level playing field, despite its southern roots. But even when we were often the first-and-onlies, Karan and I built a deeply satisfying life around our family and community of friends. We always knew we had each other's backs. Ours is a very traditional marriage, but it's also a partnership of equals. I don't think that's contradictory. A loving, supportive mate is an aspiring businessperson's most valuable asset.

After graduating from OSU, I entered Stanford University in Palo Alto, California, for graduate studies in economics. I later found out that Stanford was the alma mater of Dean Swearingen, and that he was behind my getting in the school and receiving financial aid. He had called their business school and told them, "I have this student—I think you want him out there." Because of his influence, I received an Eichler Fellowship to work towards my PhD in economics. It was an impressive honor, and it meant about three thousand dollars a year—barely enough to cover books and tuition.

During Christmas break, I gave Karan a diamond ring. We waited a year to marry because I was at Stanford and she had to finish her degree.

I didn't have a car and I didn't know how I was going to get back to Kansas for my wedding. I took a job at the post office to make some extra cash. While working there, I met a man who offered me the use of his new Volkswagen to make the trip. Another worker asked if he could pay me to take his girlfriend to Kansas because she needed to be in Illinois for a wedding and it would save her some money and time. I agreed. I didn't know she was white. As Karan later stated, it's a wonder I didn't get lynched . . . but I've rarely been stopped for "driving while black," harassed by security officers, or followed in stores. Maybe it's because I always chose to dress in business clothes.

Karan and I have many goals in common and we share a hardworking, midwestern ethic. We've wanted to accomplish so many things and to have a good, strong marriage. That first year in California, we purposely did everything together— even trips to the beauty shop and barbershop. Karan wanted a big family, but I wanted just two children to be sure I could support them and give them the things we thought they should have. I convinced my wife that this was best, but she started talking to our kids about grandchildren when they were ten! She wants a minimum of six grandchildren from our two children. (So far, we only have one grandson.)

In the early 1960s, marriage was considered more important for women than work, but I have never underestimated my wife's skills and intelligence. It was rare enough at that time for black women to earn a college degree, and Karan had even put herself through school. That took hard work, good grades, and two extra years. Although I knew it would mean she would be giving up her own dreams of a career, I told Karan that I wanted to put her at the center of our family. She would be like the center of a wagon wheel, and the kids and I would be the spokes. She would be the nucleus that would hold it all together.

Other than teaching for a short time in Teaneck, New Jersey, Karan focused her considerable talents and discipline on keeping our home, raising our children, and making sure our guests were always comfortable. She was always there for the children when I couldn't be, and she is still. Today, however, we see parents letting others raise their children— and then they're unhappy when the kids don't turn out the way they would have liked.

Karan and I have been together for forty-four years, and our love for each other is deeper than ever. She and the kids

Business in Her Blood

I earned my MBA from Duke. It was a top-ten business school at the time. It teaches the concepts of business strategy but not the day-to-day operations and how to get all the vendors and how business works. No, school doesn't tell you any of that. So if you don't have a mentor or somebody to teach you, it's a problem. I've always had my father as my mentor, and I've always valued that. However, I don't pick his brain as much anymore—probably not as much as I should—because he raised an independent black woman who can do things on her own.

I'm happiest when I'm building a company. After working at Sara Lee, then Xantus, and then as executive director of the Black MBA Association, I went out on my own. My plan is to build several businesses. I'm currently CEO at Miragent, a telecom company that I own with my brother and some other partners. Eventually, I'd like to bring someone in to replace me, so I can move on to the next challenge.

Oh, of course, I want to get married. I want to have kids, but I'm almost forty, and I'm like, "Okay, God, are you going to do this for me or not?" I don't want to get married to somebody that doesn't love me unconditionally. I've got to be with somebody who can understand who I am and what I'm about and can work with me towards my goals. One day I would love to own lots of small businesses and have them make money for me, but also be able to raise my family. That would be my vision and goal. I don't know if I'm going to get there, but we'll see. If it doesn't happen, I'm at a place in my life where, okay, if I don't get married, what's the issue? I still may raise a kid. I may not bear a kid, but I still may raise a kid.

—*Anica Howard, CEO, Miragent Communications*

have supported me in so many ways, and Karan is still my most valued adviser. She is now working on her own business interests in real estate and other investments.

Honesty, fair dealing, and sharing have always been paramount in our family. Karan sometimes got upset with me because I would help someone who asked for it, even if we had only five dollars for food for the week. I often gave away three of our five dollars. But God always provided somehow, and we never were without the things we needed.

When I insisted that we return to that Kmart store several miles away in order to return the ten dollars the cashier had mistakenly given us, Karan never raised a word of protest. At the time, we could have used that money. But she knew it was more important to me that the Howard name never bore a smudge.

I borrowed my uncle's car every day to attend class. After we were married, I was finally able to afford my own car— my first. We paid five hundred dollars for a '53 Ford that required popping the clutch to start. The couple who sold it to us liked us a lot, and they felt bad every time it broke down. It lasted six months.

Stanford gave me an invaluable education in economics. I learned everything from free enterprise to Keynesian economics to Marxist theory, and the strengths and weaknesses of each. As much as I respected one of my Marxist professors, I came to appreciate that Marxism is a system doomed to failure because it offers no incentives. It seemed to me that the basic idea behind socialism is that we are all victims of a society based on conflict, and none of us is answerable to our own fate. My life was telling me a different story.

In his book *Perestroika*, Mikhail Gorbachev wrote that his country suffered from dropping economic growth rates; ineffective quality control; indifference to scientific and technological advancement; slow (or no) improvement in living conditions; and difficulties in the supply of foodstuffs, housing, and consumer goods and services. His society had guaranteed full employment. It didn't matter how many times you were dismissed from jobs for laziness, you were always promised another. Yet this "problem-free" society, where health care and education were provided without cost, backfired. Today there is no more wage-leveling in the country, and Russia is desperately trying to establish a more capitalistic system.

Sometimes I think critics of free enterprise have the wrong idea. The reason our system works isn't greed, or selfishness. It's not "every man for himself—and to heck with the other guy." Far from it. Free enterprise is the most cooperative system there is. It is true that free enterprise relies on self-interest, but it is equally dependent on a certain kind of faith. Free enterprise assumes that if you give it your best shot, people will honor that and reward it. It demands mutual respect and rewards hard work, sacrifice, and a good product. It requires faith in one's self.

Best of all, free enterprise isn't just some big, abstract economic theory. It is based on the hardest facts of life, and at its best, the highest aspirations. Cooperation and interdependence are what make the whole thing go.

I'm living proof of that. At each important juncture in my life, someone was willing to give me a chance . . . not a favor, not an advantage, just a chance.

That's not to say there are no disappointments, setbacks, or even injustices under free enterprise. If there's an economic system that abolished all of those in actual practice, I've never heard of it.

The beauty of free enterprise, when it's allowed to work, is that no man or woman is ever counted out. You get to keep coming back. The fight's never over till you quit. In a free society, even failure has dignity. I hope I'm proof of that. We only learn from our failures—success teaches nothing.

When I was one year into Stanford's PhD program, the General Electric Company offered me a job. GE courted me for some time before I agreed to go into the business community's premier financial management program, then called Business Training Course (BTC). For three years I worked in GE's nuclear electronics products section, while taking finance and accounting courses at night. As part of my job rotation, I learned to program computers, and I eventually designed the financial management system for the division that transmitted information to corporate headquarters in New York.

By that time we were living in San Jose, California, and Karan had given birth to our daughter, Anica Lynne. I didn't yet have much time to spend with them. That fall, GE had an internal competition for a White House Fellowship. The division's chief financial officer suggested I apply since GE was screening its employees for candidates to recommend. They selected me and an employee from New York.

When I was interviewed by a regional commission in San Francisco, I was asked all kinds of questions, including some about the Vietnam War. The year was 1966, and the president was Lyndon Johnson. I replied frankly that I was opposed to the war and that I didn't think the United States should be the world's policeman. As we left the interviews, Tom Cronin, also a regional finalist and subsequent White House fellow who went on to become a prize-winning political writer and president of Whitman College, told me I probably blew it.

But I had had strong feelings about the war, and African American participation in it, for years. In a 1960 essay, "If There Were a Law," I'd written:

Negroes have found special significance in the war. It has
given us opportunities as never before, but it has sharp-
ened our sense of the clash between American creed and
American practice . . . We are no longer satisfied with the
epitaph suggested by one Negro rookie: "Here lies a black
man killed fighting a yellow man for the glory of the
white man." Negroes want to help fight, but we want
democracy to win at home too.

A second, final interview in Washington, D.C., was the
occasion of my first-ever airplane flight, which took me from
San Francisco to the East Coast. We finalists were told we'd
receive a letter informing us whether or not we'd been
accepted. I went to the Civil Service Building to pick up my
letter, then walked outside and sat on a bench to open the
envelope. My one sentence letter read, "You have been
selected as a White House fellow." I was to report immediately
to the White House! My outspokenness had not destroyed this
opportunity after all.

It was an incredible experience. I worked with former
United States Supreme Court Justice Arthur Goldberg,
who'd stepped down from the court to become the United
States ambassador to the United Nations. Some thought he
might become a vice presidential candidate with President
Lyndon Johnson, but then Johnson declined to run for
re-election. It was also thought that Goldberg might help
resolve the Vietnam conflict with the help of the U.N., if
Dean Rusk, Robert McNamara, and McGeorge Bundy
couldn't resolve it in Washington. Like Goldberg, all had
been appointed to President John F. Kennedy's cabinet.
But it seemed all the king's horses couldn't put Vietnam
together again.

I learned many invaluable lessons from Arthur
Goldberg. In our work with the U.N., the United States
mission attempted to pass many resolutions. Goldberg
taught me the value of always preparing the first draft—
because you'll usually end up getting about eighty percent

of what you want. In business, many people are simply too lazy to do the work. If you write the first draft, you may not get everything you want, but you'll be sure to be at the table.

I also learned a big lesson about tolerance. Arthur Goldberg taught us that if foreign factions were criticizing us, especially in public, very often they were doing it for their constituents back home. They may not even mean what they're saying, so there's no point in taking any of it personally. It's all politics. You learn to just listen to it, and if they vote your way or treat you positively in business affairs, leave it at that.

I would go to work at six o'clock in the morning and get home at eleven each evening. I usually went to work at the U.N., but sometimes I'd take the shuttle to Washington and drive back home to Riverdale, New York, where we lived. Karan didn't want to live in Manhattan. She said that as long as she could walk out the door and see grass in the yard, she would be happy.

One night after I came home from a weeklong trip with the White House fellows, my young daughter was still awake and didn't even recognize me. For months she'd been asleep when I left for work and asleep when I got home. I felt bad, and I was glad Karan was there for me and for our daughter.

Karan and I made a lot of good friends then, and we still keep in touch with some friends from GE, IBM, and even an army general. It was a great year, even though I only earned about twelve thousand dollars. We went in the hole for that experience, but it was well worth it.

After the White House fellowship, I took a job at Howard University as director of computer education and computer services. It was 1968, and I proposed to make Howard University the center of academic computing for the entire D.C. area. My contacts with GE and the Health Education and Welfare Department (HEW) brought promises of

discount equipment and governmental backing. I felt
strongly that computers were the wave of the future and
thought that linking Howard to the public school system
would ensure computer literacy for African Americans in the
coming millennium.

It was my shortest tenure at any job. Howard's administration was suspicious that someone just twenty-eight years
old would be able to handle such an ambitious program.
I don't believe they wanted to get involved in such a
program anyway.

The advent of the personal computer in 1980 revolution-
ized the global economy far beyond even my imagination. I
sometimes wonder how focusing on computers might have
benefitted Howard University students and helped address
what is today called the technology gap between minorities
and whites.

I left to pursue other opportunities after just nine
months at Howard. That's been another hallmark of my
career. Once it's clear that a job won't take you where you
want to go, move on. The situation is not likely to change
just because you wish it would.

I also believe that you should never ask for a raise.
Negotiate hard for what you want when you're offered a job,
and if you do it well, you should be rewarded when your work
is recognized. If you're making your goals but you're never
recognized, start looking around for the next opportunity.

In the meantime, we'd brought our son, Samuel
Howard II, whom we called Buddy, into the world. Karan
and I began discipline at the baby stage and never experienced the terrible twos. We were not cruel, but our children
learned very early what was a "no-no," which meant "don't
touch." If they began to cry, we'd send them to the "crying
room," which was the bathroom. Once they were through
crying and felt better, they would come back and join other
people. We would just point toward the bathroom, and

without saying a word they would head for it. That way we were able to think and hold conversations, and the kids could release their frustrations.

The end of my work at Howard University marked the end of one stage in my career and the beginning of another.

A Son's-eye View

I was the discipline-challenged one; Anica was the good girl. I was always the one with issues. I was the one who always had to mess with things. I remember once I wanted to learn how to cut hair—so I took some scissors to our shag carpeting.

Yes, [our parents] were spankers. They were old-school. I know now it's not acceptable, but I never was hurt by it. I always knew I was loved.

Growing up, it used to hurt me that Dad was never at any of my sporting events. Later, I realized everything he was giving up for us—and that it was for us.

I was at the Chicago Stock Exchange when he called, saying he needed my help with Xantus. There was never any question—I left that job immediately and came down the next weekend. I stayed as long as he needed me.

I've got my own business now, doing investments for a client list that includes several pro athletes. I prefer good, solid stuff to flashy risks: Give me a dry cleaner or cleaning business any day. Dad likes to help these kinds of businesses— I'm trying to be one.

I'm successful enough. But I might do some things differently when my wife and I have kids. I'm not sure my family believes me, but I could see myself becoming a house husband and staying home with the kids.

—*Buddy Howard, CEO, Knight Advisors*

I was ready to take my education in economics and my experience with government into the private sector, where I hoped I could begin achieving my dreams of business success.

Even if the world wasn't ready for a black business executive, I was ready to become one.

CHAPTER 4

THE COLLEGE OF LIFE

> Blessed is the man who walks not in the counsel of the wicked, nor stands in the way of sinners, nor sits in the seat of scoffers; but his delight is in the law of the LORD, and on his law he meditates day and night. He is like a tree planted by streams of water, that yields its fruit in its season, and its leaf does not wither. In all that he does, he prospers.
>
> —Psalm 1:1–3 (RSV)

I had been out of school for almost seven years. In spite of what I'd been told, I was beginning to find that business opportunities were available to someone with my background, no matter the color of my skin. That doesn't mean I didn't encounter racism, but if I'd listened to that man in the registrar's office at OSU, I wouldn't have been prepared when the doors of business opportunity began to open.

I've often thought that there's a College of Life that you enter after you finish your schooling. In the College of Life, every four years of life represent a year of academic training. It takes sixteen years to complete your studies in the College of Life, or twenty, if you change majors too often. So if you get out of school at twenty-four, you'll be forty by the time you have a College of Life degree. Your teachers are everyone you come in contact with. You are tested regularly, and your grades are determined by how well you learn from your experiences. If you want to know your score on the final, look at your paycheck.

You may hope you will experience only success. But the fact is that you'll never learn anything if you do nothing but succeed. All your choices, both good and bad, are building blocks of the future.

I was discouraged at the end of my Howard University experience, but another opportunity soon presented itself. I flew to New York, where I joined Thomas A. Wood, whom I call the Jackie Robinson of business. He was the first African American to take a company public, and as far as we both know, the first elected to a corporate board, that of Chase Manhattan Bank. His company name was his monogram: TAW.

As vice president of TAW International Leasing, I worked out the agreements for leasing heavy-duty road-building equipment to African countries. Historically, every time you wanted to make a deal in a developing country you'd have to go to the Overseas Private Investment Corporation (OPIC) for approval. OPIC guarantees overseas corporate investments, covering political and business risk. What we wanted was a blanket guarantee for every lease we made without having to get approval every time. In other words, we wanted to establish leasing as a business. It took over a year, but we were eventually able to obtain a blanket guarantee for leasing equipment with any country that had an OPIC arrangement with the United States. We raised ten million dollars for the initial capital.

So my first shot at being a business entrepreneur was negotiating financing and guarantee agreements for TAW's capitalization and operations along with Alan Dynner, still one of the best lawyers I know. At the negotiation table, we had OPIC's lawyers, Prudential's lawyers, an investor who'd put up two million dollars, Dynner, and me. We finally wrote

Thomas A. Wood: "The Jackie Robinson of Business"

I was probably the first black company owner to take his company public, back in 1964. I was the first black on the board of a major corporation, Chase Manhattan Bank, in probably 1972. Before I started TAW International Leasing, and worked with Sam, I was in the computer field. My company wrote programs to predict the outcome of the '64 election. We did real-time programming for the lunar module. Our biggest customer was RCA.

When I took the company public in '64, I was a neophyte. Later, someone told me: "There's a rumor on the street that's squelching your stock. The rumor is that the head of your company is a Negro." Of course, that one was true. In those days, people would walk onto an airplane and leave if they saw a black pilot. Every generation says, "I had it harder than my children." So the stock was depressed—I couldn't fight that.

We had a contract to do work for the Apollo 4 mission simulator. We told them, "This is new; it will have bugs." But there were so many problems getting it to work that there were nearly fistfights between the software and hardware people. This was back in the day when there were five thousand programmers in the whole country. We knew our programs were working. We went to see the head of the hardware company in Connecticut. I said, "You know that your machine is not working and ours is, so why do you keep accusing our work of being the problem?" He said, "I thought I would accuse you, and you would accuse me, and no one would believe you, because you are a Negro. I had to save my company."

It's just like in football: If you run a play at left tackle, and it works, do it again. If race is a weakness, it doesn't matter whether they're prejudiced or not, they'll use it. That's life.

I went to Africa, in part, because I thought I could compete on a more level playing field there. But that didn't turn out to be true. Colonial forces meant whites had more power.

We leased anything that involved earth-moving, mainly trucks. We also had a creosote factory, which impregnates wood for railroads, in Uganda; a nursing home in Kenya; a bowling alley in Nairobi; and we even leased furniture for Club Med on the Ivory Coast. We didn't anticipate it, but we ended up in fourteen countries, half French- and half English-speaking. We ended up getting a lot of Africans into businesses they wouldn't have had the opportunity to enter otherwise. I had a lot of adventures, including meeting Idi Amin.

I was very much impressed with Sam. In those days, you didn't find many financial people in our community. Some people excel in mathematics or finance, but they have no heart for it. He has compassion for the numbers; it's like a love affair. That's the kind of person you want in charge of something. He knew what the overall strategy was, and excelled. He's also extremely loyal. I wanted a black person to be in control, to sympathize with the African people and come up with innovative solutions. And that's what he did.

There are two ways to go into business. Some people go into business politically—they have a mandate, and the business comes up underneath. Sometimes they do it by building a better mousetrap. In those days, we had trouble raising money to build the mousetrap. We're now beginning to do both.

The playing field is much more level now. The challenges are more like the usual challenges of doing business. Most people don't realize how much of yourself it takes to be successful; it exacts a pound of flesh. And most businesses fail. As I like to put it, freedom is also the freedom to fail. It's the opportunity to try it. There's no guarantee that you're going to succeed, much less to succeed and endure.

Many pedestrian businesses are the core of this country, and a lot of university-trained people would look down their noses at them. I had an English teacher in New York who said, "I can teach you about life. If you want to become a millionaire, don't go to college. You go to any community, and the sanitation people have the biggest houses in town." I was the first black member of YPO [Young Presidents Organization], which then required that you had five million dollars in business. You listen to their stories. Many of these people own the basic businesses that make this country work. One fellow made shower curtains. He said, "You may laugh but my whole life is around shower curtains—the rods, the hooks—this is my whole life." He was passionate about it.

I'll be seventy-nine in January [2005]. I was in Washington for the opening of the American Indian museum. The Indians have had a much different struggle than African Americans, such as dealing with the genocide of seventy million of their people. They call Christopher Columbus's visit the "encounter," not the "discovery." They may have won battles, but they lost the war. In the museum, they have chosen not to talk about all the battles and fights. They have chosen to make the museum a celebration of the victories and the culture. That's the way I choose. I choose not to focus on the bad things that happened, because it would make me bitter. I got that from my mother.

—Thomas A. Wood,
executive and entrepreneur (retired)

a complex deal that would solve the equity and debt and guarantee the insurance.

My boss, Tom Wood, had a lot of confidence in the team. When I took our deal into him, he didn't even read it. He just signed it.

Tom and I became partners, and we're still good friends. He was my next mentor, and he taught me to always have humility and integrity in a corporate setting.

I used to go to Africa every three or four months to our offices in Kenya, Ivory Coast, Uganda, and Zambia. My first trip was to Zambia in 1968. I worked with the Zambian government as a computer consultant in strategic planning. The work day was from 8:00 A.M. to noon, then off for lunch until about 4:00 P.M., then work ended about 7:00 or 8:00 P.M. I lived in a hostel with a community bath for two months. I was supposed to be in the hostel for one week, but I came down with the mumps and was quarantined there! Nevertheless, I enjoyed working in Africa. Simply living in an environment in which blacks are the majority instilled self-confidence and pride.

After four years I decided to make a go of it on my own, and I tried to interest Tom in the radio broadcasting business. When he declined, I left TAW International with the intention of becoming the owner and operator of a number of radio stations—my first solo entrepreneurial venture.

As usual, Karan took it in stride when I announced that I would be going into an entirely new line of business. That woman could turn on a dime—if I told her money was going to be tight for a while, she could make hamburger taste like steak. I started working out of our basement, and Karan went to work as a teacher in Teaneck, New Jersey.

Market research told me that buying a radio station would be a good investment. In fact, I learned there had not been a capital loss in the radio business in twenty-five years. I formed a new company to buy radio stations and called it Phoenix Communications Group, Inc., after the mythical Egyptian symbol that meant so much to me. The phoenix represented for me not only the Christian ethos of everlasting life but also the journey I wished to make from my own humble beginnings.

I drove all over the country in our '66 Ford, visiting radio stations and just sitting and talking to everyone about what was involved in operating them. WVOL in Nashville came on the market, and I tried to buy it from Robert Rounsaville. I secured the backing of Salomon Brothers, Citibank, and Morgan Guaranty, the best bankers in the business. We did not close because Salomon Brothers did not secure the equity financing needed—I suspected a black executive in the firm kept blocking the deal! Perhaps jealousy had something to do with it. I didn't let that discourage me, and I kept looking.

I discovered over dinner with my lawyer, Jim Gammon, that the FCC had available frequencies. I found one that served the Topeka, Kansas, market (Karan's home territory). To start the station in Topeka I brought in three partners, my brother-in-law Marvin Wilson, a physician; Walt Cobler, an accountant; and Robert Bundy, an investment broker. I maintained the largest share so that Marvin and I had controlling equity. I've always been more successful in ventures in which I've been able to take an active role, as opposed to more passive investments like stocks.

In 1971 we obtained a license to broadcast in Topeka. That meant we had to build a station within a year.

I developed a plan to automate the station so it could be run with minimum staff and maximum control of the music. I'd always felt a radio station should focus on playing music, that the DJs should give the weather, the time, and maybe a little news, then shut up and get back to the music. I attended the National Association of Broadcasters meeting in Houston that fall and bought everything we needed for a fully automated radio station. A Schaefer automation

Financial Responsibility Goes Along With Social Responsibility

I came to Meharry in 1961 to set up the department of psychiatry. I thought I'd be there seven years, but by 1968 I had been asked to be president. So I never left.

In 1961, Nashville was still very much two societies. Segregation was everywhere, and it was accepted. But the students were protesting.

The interstate came in around 1968, cutting through our area and making it more difficult for us to serve people in the neighborhood. We are as much a service organization as a hospital for the area. It did aggravate our problem. It also further divided the two societies, so that people on the other side of town did not come to Meharry and did not spend their money here.

Meharry started in 1876, but its main problem in the first twenty-five years was its lack of a hospital. Later on, a doctor gave Meharry his clinic, and it became a hospital. By the time I came along, the main problem was that we didn't have enough money.

I remember when I first met Sam. I just really thought that he was unbelievably qualified for what we needed. Morally, he was the kind of person people think don't exist anymore. His integrity was unbelievably high. I couldn't believe he'd gotten from the middle of Oklahoma to be a White House fellow; I had never seen such a person.

It was critical to develop confidence in large-scale fund-raising at the school. We needed a complex, new financial system. At that point, when you come across a person like Sam, you have to believe part of it is luck and part of it is . . . Well, you have to decide that God is probably in there, too.

One of the greatest things Sam did for us was to create financial accountability. People felt good about investing in the school because they knew it would be used for what it was meant for. Over the years, we raised eighty-eight million dollars for construction, in thirteen major building projects. Two of those were major renovations; the rest were from the ground up.

I was impressed that Sam was able to take care of things so we would always have a clean audit—even when money was tight. There were very few suggestions from the auditors. I became very aware of that after Sam went on to another job—it was different later.

Sam was also a good teacher. He taught others the financial responsibility that goes along with social responsibility. He was very flexible too, because during that period we were starting a community health center that had a different structure. Sam was able to go along with whatever we were trying. I just really appreciated that. Of course, that was the primary thing he brought to the administration.

What I think Sam probably learned from me was to be concerned about people's feelings. Being a psychiatrist, that's second nature for me. When Sam went to bigger corporations, he carried that compassion with him—and still does. It's missing in many people in financial businesses.

I followed Sam's career closely. I'm sure he created Xantus because of his commitment to provide care, treatment, and prevention to people, as well as have a system that works for both the working poor and the unemployed poor. It was a great opportunity.

—*Dr. Lloyd Elam, former president,*
Meharry Medical College, Nashville

system and huge carousel for taped playlists would allow me to put my plan into action.

All told, we put less than $25,000 equity into the equipment and building of the station. The rest was a bank loan. We hired an engineer and a general manager, and we hired Washburn University students to play the tapes and read the news. Based on our simple theory that our listeners wanted to hear country music and minimal chatter, KTPK eventually became number one in the market. It required little time on my part after we got it going, and we kept it until I sold my interest in 1982 for $325,000.

I had been on Wall Street trying to court investors for that first venture when I first got a call from Dr. Lloyd Elam, president of Nashville's Meharry Medical College. He was looking for a vice president of finance and business at the school, but I put him off because I wanted to get Phoenix off the ground. He waited nine months before trying again, and then I was ready to consider his offer, which would eventually lead me into another industry: health care.

Established in 1876, Meharry was among the nation's premier medical schools for African Americans, at one time graduating over half of the country's African American doctors and dentists. But integration, inflation, and the perennial problems that affect small, private colleges had eroded Meharry's resources. Dr. Elam was frank: Unless we could position Meharry to compete, its viability as a college was questionable.

I had no background in health care and little in academia, and I still don't know how Dr. Elam got my name. But on November 1, 1973, I accepted the job and moved my family to Nashville the following January.

Karan was apprehensive. Her only experience in the South had been accompanying her aunt and uncle to a Baptist convention. There she had seen all the obvious signs of Jim Crow she hadn't been subjected to in Kansas:

the separate drinking fountains labeled "white only" and "colored," and the separate restrooms and waiting rooms. Her mother, who remained at home in Kansas, said she prayed the whole time Karan was away that she wouldn't forget where she was and drink from the closest water fountain, causing her to be arrested or worse.

When we arrived in Nashville, we were both pleasantly surprised at the friendliness of the residents and the commingling of the races. As is true of many once-segregated southern cities, Nashville's black and white communities were still starkly divided by railroad tracks, but Karan and I had already begun to learn about navigating the more subtle dividing lines between those two communities. We still discuss it today as we drive from one section to another. The fact is, we were accepted in Nashville. We did, however, experience racial objection from the owner of the house we purchased in West Meade. He refused to be present at the time our real estate agent wanted to present the offer. It took several calls to HUD and calls by influential Nashvillians to solve the situation peacefully. We lived there many years and got along with our neighbors just fine.

Perhaps as a result of my experience as a White House fellow, I was able to move easily between both cultures, an ability I believe was beneficial to Meharry. Every Saturday I drove down Jefferson Street to get my hair cut at my favorite barbershop. I began to familiarize myself with Nashville's historically black section of town, and I recognized it as both an undeveloped business opportunity and an opportunity to fill some needs of the community. After much investigation and several contacts, I decided to establish a Wendy's restaurant franchise on 28th Street. This was the first mainstream fast-food restaurant investment in Nashville's black community. Incredibly, at that time you couldn't even get a fast-food burger anywhere near the black business district around Jefferson Street.

"We Were Not Crusaders"

Aladdin Industries was family owned, and CEO Victor Johnson was on the board of Meharry Medical College. We were always interested in [having our] financial and data processing people, as we called them, to help Meharry with the administration system and planning. I'd been over there many times when Sam came in as VP of planning. In 1973–74 I was president of Financial Executives Institute (FEI). I'm 99 percent sure I was the one who invited Sam to lunch. I was impressed with him as bright, articulate, knowledgeable, as someone who would go somewhere in the field. So I thought he was a natural to be the first black member of FEI.

Aladdin Industries was in a partnership to develop Metro Center, 675 acres in north Nashville that used to flood until a dike was built. It was going to take quite a bit of marketing to make it an attractive spot. As a marketing device, Aladdin came up with the idea of buying a railroad car. It had a living room, kitchen, dining room, reception, and private chef. The rumor was that it was [Woolworth heiress] Barbara Hutton's car. It was permanently parked there—a great place to have a business lunch.

In 1974, when we had the lunch, you did not see blacks in significant positions in banks, insurance, or manufacturing. But it wasn't our intent to change that, specifically. We were not crusaders. I identified Sam as an up-and-comer with good financial acumen, who was clearly going to move forward. He had the credentials to be a member of FEI, regardless of his color.

I knew he was going to be successful, but I think I underestimated his abilities to make the jump from CFO to CEO. I would never have guessed he would have become president of the Chamber of Commerce. Sam exceeded my expectations.

—*Don Williamson, former CFO, Aladdin Industries,*
now president and CEO, Rogers Group, Inc.

After its success, several other fast-food businesses followed, but Jefferson Street continues to need rejuvenation. I later created a development of upscale homes in Bordeaux. I lost money but improved the neighborhood. One day, someone will be able to capitalize on this upscale real estate development, so close to downtown, the farmer's market, and other conveniences.

I believe that Nashville is proving to be one of the best Southern cities for African American businesspeople. Historically, it's always been a center for elite black society, thanks to Fisk University, TSU, and Meharry. By the time I arrived, businesspeople were actively seeking potential black leaders, because they knew they needed to compete with Memphis, Birmingham, and Atlanta. As time goes on, the great migration of the early part of this century has reversed, and African Americans from the northeast are finding southern cities like Nashville an attractive, open environment for business.

Meharry Medical College was my first experience in health care and my first opportunity to manage a large staff. About two hundred employees were under my direction. When I began working there, I was astonished to find that the books were kept in actual ledger books. Gordon Jones, whom I'd brought with me from TAW, and I had to start from scratch, computerizing all financial records.

In the beginning, of course, it was all a nightmare because we had to work through innumerable bugs. If anything were wrong, The System, as it came to be known, would spit out the document. One employee's husband even wrote a poem about it, with a stanza that went:

> A person of high position filled out a requisition
> And said of The System, "I hate it!
> 'Cause I sent for some glue but it didn't get through
> Maybe The System ate it."

Eventually, however, The System worked perfectly, which was essential for the task at hand. We had to put Meharry on solid financial footing and expand the physical plant in order to keep the school going.

It would be my first experience in making a public service–oriented institution, such as Meharry's hospital, cost effective. As Gordon and I recently discussed, people often think nonprofits don't make money. But they must generate surpluses, or they can't buy equipment or maintain what they need. Doctors knew they could be sued if they didn't do everything to save a patient's life, no matter the cost. We had to negotiate a number of issues, but thanks to Dr. Elam, compassion and patients' needs always ranked first. His lesson was an important one, and I will carry it with me for the rest of my life: Empathy for the disadvantaged. To Lloyd Elam, no health care system is worth much if it overlooks the poor. He was right.

It was up to me to find a way to make the numbers work— and I did.

In my four years at Meharry we were able to put $100 million of investment into the school. The Elam administration, which consisted of Ralph Hines, Lloyd Elam, and me, presided over the construction of the Basic Science Building, Dental Building, and a new tower for Hubbard Hospital.

I began to realize that it was in the field of health care that I might be able to accomplish more than simple accumulation of wealth and business success. I might be able to make a difference in people's lives, especially those who couldn't do for themselves. I might be able to do *well* by doing *good*. The promise of this mission excited me more than any business proposition I'd ever considered.

When I'd been in Nashville for less than a year, three businessmen—Jack Anderson, CEO of Hospital Affiliates; Don Williamson of Aladdin Industries; and Jack Fox of First American—invited me to lunch. This pivotal moment of my

Jack Anderson Details Success, Work, and Mentoring Sam

I was born in Mansfield, Ohio. My parents divorced when I was three or four years old. I was placed in an orphanage for a while, then in a foster home with the Anderson family, who later adopted me after I joined the navy when I was eighteen. I wasn't particularly aware of being an orphan; I had a comfortable existence. I was the only child who lived with them. They were fine parents and gave me whatever opportunities were available.

I'm proud to be called Sam's mentor. I'm also proud that he says that I helped teach him the importance of compassion in the health care business. There are very few successful businesspeople who don't understand that there are many underprivileged people. There are vast amounts of talent all over America who have not had opportunities. As a society, and as a company, and as individuals we can help those people. We help the citizen, and we help the nation. I think that's true of all successful businesspeople.

At Hospital Affiliates, we were continually looking for young managers to fill the ranks of our company. We'd been looking all over and somebody told me we had a person in Nashville who was outstanding in education and experience. He turned out to be Sam Howard.

Ideally, we were looking for people who had experience not necessarily just in hospitals, but other industries and businesses, and had an advanced degree from a good college. Sam had all of that, plus experience in Washington. The hospital gets 30 to 40 percent of its revenue from government programs. It was helpful to have people who were comfortable talking to political appointees and government people.

Sam is articulate, thoughtful, and doesn't jump to a conclusion; he thinks through the issues. He's had the advantage of an outstanding education and a well-balanced variety of business experience. In other words, he possessed all of the underpinnings you look for in management and in your own individual path for success.

It was the '70s, yes, but more important, here was a man with the education, background, and experience that we had been looking for. We were delighted to find such a person and convince him to join our organization. It was neutral in that respect—we weren't looking for someone black to join us.

It's worth noting that Sam became a business executive back in the time when minorities were disadvantaged, as they still are today. He went through the process of becoming an executive as a man, not as a minority. He handled himself well, didn't have a chip on his shoulder, and was confident of his abilities. He was successful because of that. He worked hard, was conscientious in his work, and made even-handed decisions, which in most cases affected people who were not black. He was able to move in that circle in a manner that everyone respected, and they recognized that he had the talent and willingness to work. Those are all attributes that augur success.

The experience Sam got at HAI was just a continuation of the maturing process.

—Jack Anderson, former CEO (retired),
Hospital Affiliates, Inc. (HAI)

career, with three of the most respected businessmen in Nashville, signaled an effort by the majority business community to mainstream me into the city's commercial life as a fellow business leader. Significantly, the lunch was held in a private Pullman dining car, owned by Victor Johnson, owner of Aladdin Industries. All my life I had noted how railroads separated black and white communities. This railroad car meeting would help transport me—and Nashville's elite business community—into an integrated future.

Over lunch they invited me to join the Financial Executives Institute (FEI), an organization of chief financial officers and controllers who help set the country's financial policies and accounting standards. I would be the first African American member.

Not only did the local chapter of FEI accept me, they eventually made me their president. Later, I became senior vice president and director of the national organization.

Jack Anderson, one of the men at lunch that day, began recruiting me to work for him as a strategic planner. He was to be the next mentor in my life.

We accomplished a lot at Meharry during my tenure, and I learned a lot, too. It wasn't part of my job, but I would regularly fly to Washington, D.C., to be sure our needs were included in government funding. That was valuable experience for anyone who wished to work in health care.

I recently found a letter I'd written, containing a list of suggestions on how to permanently put Meharry on better footing. Today, nearly every one of them has been implemented, including my rather bold (at the time) suggestion that we ask the federal government to forgive our debt. President Reagan would later do exactly that.

After four years at Meharry, however, it was clear that I'd progressed as far as I could. Jack Anderson offered me a job at Hospital Affiliates, Inc. (HAI). I underwent a solid year of interviews with HAI, meeting with each of the company's founders. I would be the first high-level black executive at the firm. I guess they needed to make sure I didn't have horns. The offer was an outstanding opportunity, but

"When He Knew He Was Right, He Kept Fighting"

I believe it was 1976 when Hospital Affiliates merged with American Institutional Developers. Sam was VP of development at Hospital Affiliates, charged with researching nursing homes. He did an in-depth analysis of our division, one of the first times I'd seen that done. I was impressed.

Most of the information had to be gathered by phone calls to bankers and people who knew the industry. After the Four Seasons [nursing home] scandal in the '70s, all the capital quickly left the industry, and it was difficult to get any respect for it. Sam had finite details on the performance of the division. Most people didn't think it was performing well, but lo and behold, it was performing better than everybody thought.

Sam was all for representing the acute care industry with adequate capital and management. We've built a relationship that's lasted thirty years.

Sam and I became reacquainted when my company, Genesis Health Care Ventures, was formed in 1985. Sam was on the board. I needed health care executives who were qualified and knew the business. Plus, he was a stable personality—always necessary when you're starting a company from scratch. We went through lots of growing pains.

Based on his skill and knowledge, I loaned him one million dollars to start his company. The company didn't have any assets to speak of. I guess it was a personal loan, now that I think of it. He secured it with a pledge of the stock he held in Phoenix. I recollect he paid it back in one lump-sum payment.

Sam had started the company believing managed health care was the way to a better health care system. I saw it as an opportunity to grow Genesis. I certainly learned a lot about managed care. We used that knowledge to make investments in [other] companies and got a good return on our investment.

Sam and I have done a number of things. He was one of the initial investors in Genesis when there was no public market. And as I recall, he got cash back on his return.

I never thought, *I want a minority to work in the company.* That was never a part of the decision. The more that's a part of discussion, the less comfortable an investor is going to be, because if the person is emphasizing race, it will be a distraction from the business itself. The business is health care, and if you focus on that, everybody is going to buy it. No one is going to buy it because you're a minority. They're going to buy it because of the product.

Sam taught me to clearly articulate opportunities, goals, objectives, and plans, whether in writing or speech. He taught me how to do business planning. I have my MBA from Temple, but my business skills didn't teach me how to do business. It taught me how to write a sentence, but not how to operate a business. Sam was one of the best. When he knew he was right, he kept fighting when people told him no. That was one of the first times I'd seen senior management listen to lower management—and make money from it.

I ended up learning how to do acquisitions. Sam opened up the gate and I ran in. When that division was sold, I started another company and did acquisitions there. That was Health Group Care Centers, which later sold for multimillions. It gave me enough money for Genesis Health Centers.

No doubt, Sam opened the door. It was sort of a reverse role—he opened it for the majority. He helped a lot of young guys over the years. I wouldn't be surprised if you find a lot of that at HCA. It was part of being good executives.

There are a few good CEOs like that in the world.

—*Mike Walker, entrepreneur*

I wasn't willing to relinquish the job status I'd worked so hard to earn at Meharry. I wouldn't accept a director's position; on that I was firm. I had been vice president at Meharry, and I needed the same title at HAI.

In 1977, I became vice president of strategic planning at HAI. Jack's methodical way of introducing me to HAI's corporate structure had worked. I felt I knew everyone and everyone knew me. Although I'd worked with whites on the board and in the administration at Meharry, this was my first job outside an African American environment since working at General Electric.

Although my title at HAI was vice president of strategic planning, it was a unique situation because I actually reported to Jack, the CEO. When they hired a president, I still didn't report to him. That caused a little bit of ruffle between me and the new president. Jack would continue to talk to me because the president was down the hall and I was right next door.

Jack taught me how to work in major corporations in the United States. For four years I carried his bags; I was his assistant. I'm speaking metaphorically, of course. But he taught me a lot more about business, how business works, and how to do big deals than probably any one person that I know. Jack was my advisory professor in the College of Life. He worked my butt to death. He was rough, but I never cried. I did see people come out of his office crying, though. Once, when we had boarded a plane to Philadelphia to make a presentation, Jack had me redo the work on the flight.

In those days, some planes had one row of seats facing another in the first row. I sat right in front of Jack and he watched me. I worked my calculator to death trying to make sure I got it right. At the end, there was a penny-per-share difference; I had made a mistake. Jack was a brilliant financial person, so he could spot it.

Not a Burden, But an Opportunity

I met Sam in 1981, when he was with Hospital Affiliates. When we merged companies, I made him treasurer of HCA, a much larger company. Over the next few years, he did a wonderful job with the public as well as with banks and bondholders and insurance companies.

He was always well liked, an integral part of HCA management, and an important part of the culture of the company, as a caring compassionate provider of health care.

Sam certainly walked the talk. He lived the company's values. They were so closely aligned with his own values of loyalty, honesty, caring about others, and reaching out to others less fortunate than himself. He knew the importance of his role as one of the leading African Americans of the community, which he wore with great humility. He didn't look at it as a burden, but an opportunity to do something philanthropic. His wife, Karan, also helped him greatly.

You're always looking in any community for highly educated, attractive, smart, motivated people to take leadership roles. Sam was always at the top of any list I saw put together. He's involved in almost anything worthwhile happening in the community. Socially, also, in a very quiet, tasteful way, he opened the door for many other blacks to follow. His children went to the top prep schools and joined exclusive clubs.

Quite frankly, I didn't look at the color of his skin. I just saw him as a wonderful businessman.

—*Dr. Thomas Frist, former CEO, HCA; board chairman,*
Frist Foundation, and many other entities

Jack taught me about business and the business of health care. He took many concepts out of theory and put them into practice. HAI was the first to create the hospital management contract, an ingenious way of raising capital for hospitals. Nonprofit entities would be established to buy the hospitals, and they in turn would form long-term management contracts with HAI. These nonprofits would have access to the nontaxable bond market for financing.

Like Dr. Elam, Jack Anderson also believed in the mission involved in health care. An orphan himself, he could relate to the needy and disadvantaged.

Jack Anderson later became CEO of INA Health Care, and I remained a vice president of the group. My job as chief strategist was to grow the company, and my first strategic investment was in the health maintenance organization (HMO) business.

The first HMO we bought, in 1979, was HMO International in California. From that seed grew CIGNA Health Plans. I'm proud to say I'm the father of the CIGNA Health Plan.

Next, we focused on nursing homes. Our nursing homes had a 12 percent pretax margin, and we had people who could run them better than anyone in the industry. The strategy we developed at HAI became Genesis Health Ventures. Mike Walker, the brilliant principal financial officer of the INA Nursing Homes, developed Genesis with pharmacies, nursing homes, physicians, and rehabilitation all in one market, so the customer can be well provided for. A computer system keeps track of all their medicines and medical history and gives life-time support, called eldercare. An elderly person registers with the company, and they receive packets to take care of them for the rest of their lives. It relieves families of a lot of worry and responsibility. I'm still on the board of Genesis.

When Hospital Corporation of America (HCA) acquired HAI in 1981, I joined HCA. I met another long and solid friend, Dr. Thomas Frist, then CEO of HCA.

I was learning about the health care industry from the ground up from some of the most caring, compassionate mentors in the region, as an employee of some of the best-run institutions and corporations anywhere. In the meantime, I was still searching for radio stations to buy. While working for corporate America, I was spreading my entrepreneurial wings.

Clockwise from left: Samuel Houston Howard was named for his maternal grandfather, Poppa Sam Gaines, shown here with his wife; Howard received his middle name from his father, Houston Howard (pictured), who in turn, was named for his father; siblings Lula, Maurice, Callie, and Samuel Howard in a photo circa 1950; and Samuel Howard's mother, Nellie Gaines Howard.

Top left: Karan Anica Wilson Howard, in a photo taken about the time she and Howard met. **Top right:** Samuel H. Howard, 1962. **Bottom:** Howard pictured in the 1961 Oklahoma State University yearbook.

Samuel H. Howard and Karan Wilson married on December 29, 1962, at the Bethany Chapel Baptist Church in Ottawa, Kansas.

Top: Howard was the first General Electric employee to be selected as a White House fellow. Here, he discusses his upcoming government assignment with GE President Fred J. Borch. **Bottom:** Howard worked for U.S. ambassador to the United Nations Arthur Goldberg during his fifteen months as a White House fellow.

Top: President Lyndon B. Johnson congratulates Howard on his selection as a White House fellow, as Justice William Henry Hastie, the first African American federal judge, looks on. **Bottom:** President Lyndon B. Johnson greets Howard and other White House fellows on the White House lawn.

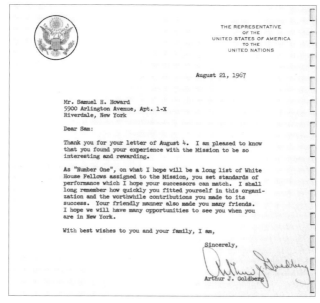

THE REPRESENTATIVE
OF THE
UNITED STATES OF AMERICA
TO THE
UNITED NATIONS

August 21, 1967

Mr. Samuel H. Howard
5900 Arlington Avenue, Apt. 1-X
Riverdale, New York

Dear Sam:

Thank you for your letter of August 4. I am pleased to know
that you found your experience with the Mission to be so
interesting and rewarding.

As "Number One", on what I hope will be a long list of White
House Fellows assigned to the Mission, you set standards of
performance which I hope your successors can match. I shall
long remember how quickly you fitted yourself in this organization and the worthwhile contributions you made to its
success. Your friendly manner also made you many friends.
I hope we will have many opportunities to see you when you
are in New York.

With best wishes to you and your family, I am,

Sincerely,

Arthur J. Goldberg

Top: The 1966–1967 class of White House fellows. Howard is on the far right, back row. **Bottom:** United Nations Ambassador Arthur Goldberg commended Howard for his work with the U.S. mission to the United Nations.

Top: Howard (far left) and others relax with Vice President Hubert Humphrey during Howard's time as a White House fellow. **Bottom:** Howard (in front row, center) at the White House with President Gerald Ford and First Lady Betty Ford in 1976.

Top left: Metro Nashville Mayor Richard Fulton and Howard at ceremonies commemorating the opening of the Metropolitan Nashville Convention Center. Howard served as commission chairman in 1986–1987 and 1993–1994; he also chaired the center's finance committee from 1988–1992. **Top right:** One of serveral corporate portraits taken of Howard during his career. **Bottom:** Samuel, Karan, Anica, and Buddy in 1977.

Top: Howard served as chairman, president, and director of the Federation of American Hospitals. Here, he and Karan are congratulated by immediate past president Henry J. Werronen and his wife in 1986. **Bottom:** Howard served as president and director of 100 Black Men of Middle Tennessee, Inc., helping and mentoring others.

Top: Howard meets with General Colin Powell, the sixty-fifth secretary of state of the United States. Powell was also a White House fellow several years after Howard. **Bottom left:** Samuel and Karan Howard before the Swan Ball, one of Nashville's premiere charity events, benefiting the Cheekwood Botanical Garden and Museum of Art. **Bottom right:** Howard in his office, 1998.

Nashville Business Journal

$1.00   MAY 15-19, 1995   TWO SECTIONS

Howard rises to the top

Phoenix Healthcare chief named Executive of the Year

By Elizabeth Niendorf

Thumbing through his little black date book, Sam Howard, chairman of Phoenix Healthcare Corp., finds a lesson he's learned in "the college of life."

"Some battles choose us," says Howard. "I don't know where I saw this, but I wrote it down April 3."

Howard, the *Nashville Business Journal* 1995 Small Business Executive of the Year, has fought plenty of battles during his career. At 56, he's enjoying victory.

It was 1957 when Howard began his freshman year at Oklahoma State University. The business student from Lawton, Okla., was told he would never succeed in the business world.

"They said 'Why don't you be a musician? Why don't you teach?'" says Howard. "But I said, 'No. I want to go into business.'"

More than 30 years later, Howard still can't wait to do business. He's usually the first one to arrive at the office, and he often comes bearing doughnuts. His first task of the day is making coffee for his employees. "And I walk around a lot," says Howard. "I believe in management by walking around."

Phoenix rising

Howard had begun thinking about a health maintenance organization for Medicaid patients when he and some friends discussed how to cut Medicaid costs. "What would happen," Howard asked, "if someone could find out the No. 1 procedure in Medicaid and save the government money?"

The answer: A thriving managed care company would emerge from the ashes of a demand-driven government program.

In 1993, Howard formed Phoenix Healthcare with three

Continued . . .

NBJ photo by Bill Thorup

Sam Howard, 1995 Executive of the Year.

Howard was named Small Business Executive of the Year by the *Nashville Business Journal* in 1995.

Top: Howard (back row, left) was appointed to the National Bipartisan Commission on the Future of Medicare by then-House Speaker Newt Gingrich. **Bottom left:** Howard was surprised by his Xantus employees with a cake and special commemorative photo album on his sixtieth birthday. **Bottom right:** A pencil sketch was part of a thank-you presentation by the Nashville Convention Center to commemorate Howard's contributions as commission chairman.

Top: This billboard was part of the marketing for Phoenix Healthcare of Tennessee, Inc., Howard's innovative managed health care company. **Middle:** Howard makes a point as Senator Bill Frist listens during meetings for the Nashville Health Care Council. **Bottom:** During Howard's tenure as chairman-elect (1997–1998), vice chairman (1995), chairman (1998–1999), and director of the Nashville Chamber of Commerce (1993–1999), Dell Computers announced it was moving facilities to the Nashville area.

Phoenix Healthcare fulfillment of a dream

By JULIE BELL
Staff Writer

Phoenix Healthcare Corp., the Nashville-based managed-care company that recently announced its expansion into Mississippi, now is launching a statewide HMO plan for small businesses in Tennessee.

The moves marks a new stage for Phoenix and its chairman, Samuel Howard. After 2¹/₂ profitable years handling TennCare, the state's Medicaid reform program, Howard wants to prove he can not only run a $52-million-a-year managed-care company but expand it into a $400 million regional force.

Phoenix, which soon will offer a Medicaid health-maintenance organization plan in 19 Mississippi counties, is reviewing opportunities in Georgia and South Carolina and launching Community Plus, the small-business plan. If it successfully diversifies, Phoenix could issue its first public stock within a couple of years, says J.C. Bradford & Co. partner Robert Doolittle.

"He's got one of the hottest Medicaid companies in America," says Jim Cooper, an Equitable Securities Co. managing director and friend of Howard. "People from all over the country already are knocking on his door.'

In some way, Howard, 57, has nothing to prove. He was treasurer at Hospital Corporation of America and Hospital Affiliates International, which HCA had acquired before it was folded into Columbia/HCA Healthcare Corp. He became nationally known in his field while president of the Federation of American Health Systems, an association representing 1,200 for-profit hospitals. He remains close to mentor/friend Thomas Frist Jr., Columbia's vice chairman.

But ever since a white fellow student at Oklahoma State University told him in

the late 1950s that blacks couldn't succeed in business, Howard has been motivated to head a major company. He long has owned radio stations — WVOL-AM in Nashville, WQQK-FM in Hendersonville and two stations in Tupelo, Miss. — but he looks to Phoenix Healthcare to fulfill his dream.

"There was no affirmative action for this," Howard says. "It was just put in your money and take your risk."

As a chief executive, Howard has continued to abide by a philosophy that calls for paying attention to little things, causing larger ones to fall into place. He still spends about four hours once a month combing through Phoenix records on everything from pharmacy utilization to births, typing results for each category into a computer spreadsheet to compare them.

The company reflects Howard's attention to detail. A sign in Phoenix's claims-processing area last week proclaimed the company was taking an average three days to pay claims, well under the state's 30-day requirement. Phoenix employees' monthly error rate while typing in claims: less than 1%.

Howard built Phoenix in part by using the connections he'd made at HCA and the Federation. Both Columbia and Community Health Systems, a Brentwood-based hospital operator, are part of Phoenix's statewide network of providers, which now

includes more than 3,000 doctor and 130 hospitals.

But TennCare's once-a year enrollment period offer limited opportunities fo growth, prompting Howard t look to more states and new products. Community Plus is forerunner to Phoenix's nex product — a Medicare HMO.

Phoenix aims to attrac 8,000 enrollees to Community Plus in the plan's first yea then add 20,000 in 1997 Brentwood-based McAlister Marketing Corp. is marketing the new plan, which features no claim forms or deductibles $10-$15 copays and free dental an vision benefits. The plan also wil experiment with making it easier fo enrollees to go to some specialist without a referral from their primary care doctor.

When Howard started Phoenix i May 1993 with TennCare looming, h had four people with HMO experience Now his young staff of 64 includes son Samuel, 27, who works in finance, an daughter, Anica Howard, 31, wh oversees Phoenix's Tennesse operations.

"If I disappear tomorrow I can fee pretty good," Howard says. "Thes young people can carry it on."

About Samuel H. Howard

Position: Chairman and chief executive officer, Phoenix Healthcare Corp.; chairman, president and chief executive officer, Phoenix Communications Group.

Career path: Senior vice president-public affairs and, previously, vice president and treasurer, Hospital Corporation of America; vice president and treasurer, Hospital Affiliates International; vice president-finance and business, Meharry Medical College; vice president-finance, TAW

International Leasing Corp.; consultant, U.S. Health, Education and Welfare Department; educational computer services director, Howard University; White House Fellow and special assistant to United Nations Ambassador Arthur Goldberg; financial analyst, General Electric Co.

Education: Stanford University master's degree in economics, 1963; Oklahoma State University bachelor's degree in business administration, 1961.

The *Tennesseean* used Phoenix Healthcare's launch of a statewide HMO plan to profile the company and its chairman.

Top: On June 15, 2001, Samuel and Karan Howard were honored to meet with President George W. Bush in the Oval Office. **Bottom:** Howard (seated, front row, left) served on Mayor Phil Bredesen's Commission on Crime in 1998.

Top left: Karan and Samuel Howard celebrate their wedding anniversary at Arthur's restaurant in Nashville. **Top right:** Samuel, daughter Anica, daughter-in-law Allyn, wife Karan, and son Buddy pose for a Howard family portrait, Easter 2005. **Bottom:** Anica, Samuel, Karan, and Buddy during ceremonies inducting Samuel Howard into the Oklahoma State University Hall of Fame in 1999. He was also inducted into the university's College of Business Administration Hall of Fame in 1983.

CHAPTER 5

FLY, PHOENIX

Look at the birds of the air: they neither sow nor reap nor
gather into barns, and yet your heavenly Father feeds them.

—Matthew 6:26 (RSV)

*M*y radio station in Topeka, KTPK, had done so well
that I welcomed the opportunity to buy another
when it became available. This time it was that
first station I had tried to buy in 1972, the R&B station in my
newly adopted hometown of Nashville, WVOL. In 1980, I
was successful.

I hadn't had to do much at KTPK once I got it going on
my automated plan, and I'd been able to keep it going
while continuing my jobs at Meharry and HAI. I didn't
think the situation would be much different in Nashville.
Besides, WVOL was already up and running with a decent
playlist. The DJs were well-known personalities, and I kept
them on. In 1982 I had the opportunity to purchase 92Q,
a general-market station in Nashville, with a bank loan
plus seller financing. When the original format floundered,
I converted 92Q to urban contemporary and moved the
operation to the building that already housed WVOL.

Karan helped immeasurably by running the stations for
a short time. Later, John Haggard ran both stations and

significantly improved operations. I eventually hired my best friend and put him in charge of the two stations. In 1984 I sold my interest in KTPK in Topeka, realizing a $325,000 profit.

I continued my career in health care at the same time. HAI was acquired from INA by HCA in 1981, and I became vice president and treasurer for them. In 1986 I was promoted at HCA to senior vice president of public affairs.

All the while, I continued my work in the community. When Hank Aaron's wife, Byllye Aaron, asked me to work with the United Negro College Fund (UNCF), I agreed to head up their local fund-raising efforts for five years. After working with Meharry for so long, I was thoroughly knowledgeable about the difficulties black colleges often encounter in raising money. The UNCF ran a telethon with Lou Rawls as its host. Historically, black colleges that were members of UNCF had to host a telethon in their communities.

The event was a smashing success, raising our goal of $125,000 on the first night. By the next year, we raised $500,000, with the help of Nashville corporations. In five years, we raised over $4,000,000.

The major benefactor was Fisk University, among the nation's most prestigious historically black colleges. As the oldest university in Nashville, with a list of brilliant alums stretching from W. E. B. DuBois to former Treasury Secretary Hazel O'Leary (who became president of Fisk in 2004), Fisk has a grand history befitting its impressive Victorian architecture. It is the mother ship of black institutions. Founded after the Civil War for former slaves, Fisk had faced down a number of crises over the years, its sons and daughters overcoming low expectations, little money, and racism by taking control of the school's destiny at critical moments. The famed Fisk Jubilee Singers are just one example—the group of student singers toured the world, raising money and awareness, when Fisk faced an early closure in the late 1800s.

In the mid-1980s, Fisk was again addressing cultural shifts, both inside and outside its brick walls. During the 1960s, demonstrations and radicals on campus had driven off many white contributors of years past. Fisk's administrators dipped into its endowment (never a wise course of action) to make ends meet. By the time Henry Ponder became president in 1984, he was told it had dwindled to $4.3 million. He was soon to discover that the school's debts amounted to around $4.7 million. There was no unencumbered money.

Students again took it upon themselves to save the school—this time, with cups on Jefferson Street, begging for donations from passersby. Fisk supporters were aghast—the university's prestigious profile was damaged. However, it was plain that Fisk was in trouble; the money the students raised went to meet monthly utility bills.

Henry Ponder called me soon after arriving at Fisk. Like me, he had been schooled in Oklahoma. Like me, he preferred action to talk. We were also members of the same fraternity, Alpha Phi Alpha, "the first of the first." Henry eventually became general president of the Alphas during his Fisk presidency.

Henry recognized that Fisk's crisis demanded a new kind of leadership, so he asked me to join Fisk's board. I was part of a team that was something of a new guard. When he had negotiated with the banks, they told him he needed new board members who reflected American business. So he brought on a number of successful businesspeople, many of whom were white, because he needed a board that could reassure the banks that we could meet Fisk's notes if necessary and because he needed the board themselves to be donors. Members of the board included Benjamin R. Rechter, a private, major business owner and investor; Peter Thombros, executive vice president of Pfizer; Richard J. Eskind, a broker and investment banker, and his wife, Jane, who had run for governor; Cecilia Atkins, who was CEO of the National Baptist Convention; and Martin Brown of Brown-Forman. I was the only African American in Ponder's new crop of pro-business board members.

Raising money is a president's job, and Henry Ponder was good at it. He actually gave more money to Fisk than anyone on the board. The old-guard board at Fisk weren't necessarily donors; yet, they made being Fisk board members

Cultural Shift at Fisk

B y the time Henry Ponder arrived at Fisk, it had already reached a crisis. College students were out on the streets, raising money with cups. Many people didn't see a social class difference among African Americans at that time, but this is a historically middle-class school. People didn't send their children to Fisk to be out with cups.

But like many in the middle class, Fisk had to begin to live above its means. The old-guard trustees would say, "Why don't you go to the Ford Foundation for donations?" Well, by the 1980s, the Ford Foundation had shifted its interest from African American education to hunger in Asia. The older trustees were caught in a time warp. Many alumni didn't even send their children back to the school.

In part, Fisk was suffering the repercussions of its involvement in the civil rights movement. Those repercussions were serious with regard to finance and business. Many whites who had supported Fisk had a fundamental difference with the idea being sought. They weren't comfortable with African Americans stepping out of their roles, or with the fundamental associate changes. At that time, it became very difficult to raise funds for an institution like Fisk.

Things changed with Sam Howard and the other members of the new board, a very politically and economically savvy group. Looking back, Sam's arrival was a part of a cultural shift that was going on at the time. Like Henry Ponder, he represented a business philosophy. Ponder had been president at Benedict College in South Carolina. He liked challenges. He felt it was a mission to save a historic college.

Old-guard trustee members at Fisk would make up business cards that said, "Fisk Trustee." They'd introduce themselves by saying, "Hello, I'm Reavis Mitchell, member of the board of Fisk." You don't know who's on the board at Harvard. You don't know who's on the board at Vanderbilt. You didn't know the new board at Fisk, but the old guard always brought that out.

Henry Ponder could get you in a room—he was six feet one. It seemed like he was about six feet five. He could get you in a short handshake, and he could talk to you about his project. And he brought in a lot of money.

But he had very little tolerance for people who wasted money, made bad investments, or would encourage a college president to make bad investments. So, with the help of the new board members, we restored the buildings. We made the UNCF drive work. Sam chaired the committee that selects people for the board. We ran meetings like clockwork. He ran the meetings like he ran his business. We got the board meetings down from two-and-a-half days to an evening-and-a-half. But Sam never invited them to his house. And on one occasion, probably because he was going the other way, he declined to give some board members a ride to where they were going in his Jaguar. You know how it is when you aren't invited—the place you aren't invited to takes on more grander, more regal dimensions.

—Dr. Reavis Mitchell, chairman,
History Department, Fisk University

a kind of full-time job. Our board meetings used to last two or three days—far longer than necessary. I shortened them. I agreed to one retreat, where a consultant prepared a PowerPoint presentation emphasizing the need for each board member to donate. Many seemed to be on the board simply to socialize. Yet any board, especially one at an endangered black university, has as its first priority a fiduciary responsibility.

To me, this is the essence of why American business has proved to be a better leveler of the playing field than any protest or affirmative action program. To make a dream come true, you have to make the numbers work.

I became Henry Ponder's closest associate on the board, and I made some unpopular decisions. We had too many students who weren't paying their bills; I said that had to stop. That resulted in the students taking over the library in a protest, but we stuck it out. Fisk was a school, not a charity.

After several very successful years, the board—mainly the old guard—decided not to renew Henry Ponder's contract. That turned out well for him, and he went on to better things. But the new guard of trustees left, one by one. I left, too, because I knew it would be an uphill battle to continue to work with the old guard. Besides, our work was done. We'd saved the school. However, Fisk's endowment, as far as I know, hasn't had any major contributions in years.

Today, I think Fisk and Meharry should merge. It would be a hard sell politically, but it would benefit both institutions, putting them on financially firm footing.

In the meantime, during my years with UNCF and Fisk, my career was continuing unabated. In 1989 I decided to resign from my position at HCA, as the company was beginning to divest itself of hospitals, forming companies like HealthTrust and Quorum. I wanted to become more involved in executive operations as opposed to finance, so I opted to focus on radio broadcasting.

I acquired two stations in Tupelo, Mississippi (WELO and WZLQ-FM)—my first bad acquisition. I overpaid the owners, who then lured away some of my key staff. I eventually sold the stations at a loss.

The Nashville stations began to perform poorly, and I had to fix the operations. The most painful task of all lay before me: After five years, I would have to replace the stations' general manager—my best friend.

If you are in charge of personnel, you must hold them accountable. And if your business is going to work, you must let go of the people who are not performing up to expectations. But as any manager knows, firing someone is difficult. Somehow it seems that you've failed too—and often that feeling is right on target. You've failed to match the right person with the right job.

I knew my friend had a family who depended on him, and I regretted that we might not remain friends. But we had to part ways.

I asked to see him first thing in the morning so that he wouldn't have to dread the meeting all day. I tried to be simple and direct, and respectful of his feelings. I believe he knew what was coming, and I didn't see the need to drag it out. Of course he was upset.

After a time, we were able to resume our friendship, and today we talk frequently. We've never spoken about what happened, however, and it hovers over both of us. I think one day we should share a couple of glasses of Crown Royal, talk it out, and I hope, clear the air so we can come to terms with that painful time.

The firing came too late to save the two stations. In fact, it soon became inescapable that I would have to take them through bankruptcy proceedings. The crisis point came when my bank decided to get out of the broadcasting lending business and asked for immediate payment of the loan. Since we could not pay it, we engaged the best lawyer in town and filed for Chapter Eleven bankruptcy.

I was mortified that my creditors hadn't been paid, and I was convinced that bankruptcy would be an indelible black mark on my credit, representing the end of my entrepreneurial endeavors. Fortunately, there was little press about the stations' failure. Still, I was embarrassed.

But I do believe that success teaches you very little, and this spectacular failure was about to teach me some of the most valuable business lessons of my life. I learned that it's possible to make a comeback in our economic system, and I learned many lessons on just how that can be done—how to reconstruct a corporation, how to work with the courts, and in general, how to work in the system to fix a big problem.

First, I set about negotiating with my local creditors. To my amazement, I found that nearly all of them dealt with bankruptcy often, and they were extremely cooperative. They knew it was in their own best interests to help me get the stations back on track so we could become regular paying customers again.

But the bank refused to negotiate with us. As a result, we had to file a bankruptcy plan on which a judge held a hearing. After two days of testimony, the judge ruled. If we would invest an additional $250,000 in the company, we could have twenty-five years to pay off the total loan.

I would later discover that bankruptcy would not keep me from finding partners or investors. In fact, entrepreneurs coming out of bankruptcy with a clean slate are often attractive to investors, who know they aren't dealing with a huge debt load.

The most difficult task by far during the bankruptcy was rescuing my investment in 92Q and WVOL. I knew they were valuable properties, and I refused to sell them at a loss. I would have to take a more active role in running the stations, and I would simply have to figure out why they weren't working.

I went back to the drawing board to come up with more profitable formats. I returned to my theory that radio audiences want to hear music, not DJs, as KTPK's success had proven. I instructed the staff in the new philosophy, and those who couldn't go along with it were allowed or encouraged to leave. I took a good, hard look at the sales staff and fired those who weren't producing. I kept the pay levels competitive, to attract and keep good salespeople. They were the engines that made the whole thing go.

To attract advertisers, we'd have to deliver an audience, and 92Q's market share had declined slowly for years. I needed to find a way to attract that audience, and I needed to be able to explain the method to others so I could hand over day-to-day operations to them.

Using a Lotus spreadsheet and my own research, I came up with a mathematical formula for producing the playlists. I gave each element in the formula a numerical weight. Listeners, I believed, wanted a reasonably short playlist—say, forty songs—and to know they could prob-ably hear a particular song every couple of hours. I based my spreadsheet on ratings from *Billboard*, *R&B*, and *Top Ten*, as well as local record store sales. (By calling the stores, we learned what was selling well—or coming up— and added that to the mix.) I'd throw in an oldie or two. "One in a Million" was something you could expect to hear fairly frequently. We would be consistent so that listeners would know what they would hear when they tuned in.

I banned any rap or suggestive music. I didn't want parents in the community unhappy about what their children were listening to, and if a mother called me to complain, I took immediate action and removed the offending song. Some might call that censorship, but there were plenty of alternatives in the market if you wanted to hear such music. My station was going to be different. It's all a matter of giving the consumer a choice.

I hired a programming director to follow my formula and keep it current with regular calls to local record shops. DJs gave the weather, the time, and some news, and then shut up to play the music.

Three programmers who worked for me each received a Programmer of the Year award for their respective markets, and they invited me to go with them to the honors banquets. I was pleased that they were recognized for implementing my plan, and proud of them for receiving the recognition they deserved. I've always believed that the job of a good leader is to devise an effective plan, and the employees who carry it out well should be honored. Besides, my own rewards were even more tangible—92Q went to number one in the market.

Before long, our profit was over $1 million a year. In 1997 I sold the stations, which I'd bought for $2.4 million of mostly other people's money, for $12 million cash. It had taken seven-day work weeks, but I'd proven to myself what I'd suspected all along: If I had control, I could make it as an entrepreneur.

Long before I sold the stations, however, I began my next venture. As it happened, all my business experience thus far had given me the perfect background for an opportunity that was laid at my feet, to fulfill my dream of matching mission with market, of doing well by doing good.

The flight of the Phoenix was about to begin.

CHAPTER 6

THE VIEW
FROM THE PEAK

Whoever seeks to gain his life will lose it, but whoever
loses his life will preserve it . . . for every one who exalts
himself will be humbled, but he who humbles himself will
be exalted.

—Luke 17:33, 18:14 (rsv)

*I*n April 1993, I was in the right place at the right time.
Stephen Braden and I had become partners and formed
a company just three months earlier in order to pursue
opportunities in public-sector health care. Then, the governor
made an announcement: Tennessee was to create an alternative to Medicaid for the Medicaid eligibles and the state's
uninsured population.

The state wanted to provide medical coverage through
managed care organizations (MCOs) rather than paying
providers directly. The MCOs would negotiate contracts
with health care providers, opening health care pricing to
the rigors of the marketplace. Tennessee had been controlling its health care costs under the Blue Cross preferred
provider organization (PPO), and the new system would
work in a similar way. The state believed that the private
sector could manage the medical services delivered to the
Medicaid and uninsured populations for less than what they
were spending on Medicaid alone.

Tennessee's Medicaid program had seen skyrocketing enrollment and costs for more than a decade, and the expenses were projected to balloon 20 percent every year for the next five years. Legislators chose not to go the usual route, which was to raise taxes and cut benefits, but instead opted for competition.

The new program was called TennCare. The state developed contracts with private managed care providers, then required Medicaid recipients to choose a plan and enroll. Tennessee would no longer be in the Medicaid business.

I immediately recognized the genius of TennCare. It was exactly what my partner and I had prepared for. Once consumers had a choice, managed care providers would have to meet their demands—and improve. Customers could hold MCOs accountable and vote with their feet (change companies) if they didn't like the company's service.

In fact, I'd authored a similar plan in 1980 while working for INA Health Care Group. I called it the Health care Options Plan Entitlement, or HOPE. Harvard economist Dr. William Hsiao prepared an economic analysis of HOPE which demonstrated that privatizing Medicare and Medicaid programs could save enough money to cover all the uninsured in America. At the time, however, the public was not ready to embrace privatizing government health care or offering choice for consumers. Medicare and Medicaid didn't offer options, and their subscribers weren't used to having them.

But I've always believed passionately in the concept of mission, and I continued to dream of doing well by doing good. I also believe that God gave me a vision of addressing the health care needs of vulnerable populations using a HOPE-style mechanism. I may not be around to see the plans put into action, but they *will be* implemented. We have already seen Medicare, Medicaid, and private plans evolve toward choice. The only missing ingredient is a flexible pricing mechanism reflecting a competitive market.

In 1993 I was ready to re-enter the health care field under TennCare. I had everything I needed to create a successful managed care company just as I'd envisioned under HOPE—everything, except start-up capital. I had expertise from working at every level in health care; I had connections (my mentors in the health care business were working at high levels to make the program work); and I was committed to TennCare's concept of insuring every Tennessean and allowing the consumer to make the choices.

I saw only one flaw in TennCare, but it was a big one. I had my firm's actuary analyze the state's capitation (per person) rates to MCOs. They didn't add up. Shortfalls might not show up right away, but they were bound to arrive eventually. And since profits were the engine that drove TennCare, this could spell doom for the entire program.

The state had applied for a federal waiver to substitute Medicaid with TennCare. So I went straight to the top and wrote to Health and Human Services Chief Donna Shalala in September of 1993. I'd detailed Tennessee's failure to adequately fund TennCare, despite its contract to do so. Attaching an analysis by my accounting firm, KPMG Peat Marwick, I wrote, "The capitation rates do not appear to be developed on an actuarially sound basis."

I never got a satisfactory response from that letter. And for the short term, TennCare would prove to be highly successful. I decided, as I had with many other business ventures, to keep working, in good faith that the market-place would reveal TennCare's flaws, and that they would be corrected.

I found excellent people to work with me. I hired my assistant, Tanya Yates (now Hausmann), on a referral from a friend. She's been tested many times, and I've always found her indefatigable in her commitment. She and

Stephen Braden were the first people I brought on, before I even had a company. I put them on the radio station payroll until we got going.

From the earliest days in managed care, I was a proponent of allowing our insured members to choose their doctors. That option gave our company an edge over many others—another example of allowing the marketplace to solve business problems.

Investing in Medicaid HMOs held no appeal for venture capitalists in 1993, so with the help of my friend Mike Walker, CEO of Genesis Health Ventures, we capitalized the company with a Bank of Nashville personal loan of one million dollars and a one-million-dollar guaranty fee to Genesis. I called my new company Phoenix Health Care Corporation, which later changed to Xantus when I learned an insurance company already held a similar name. Our employees chose the name Xantus, which means "state of well-being."

Our first task was to hammer out a contract with health care providers, so I hired a specialist expert in provider contracts. Our goal was to create a nearly statewide provider network. At a meeting with our staff, the expert declared the goal to be impossible; I dismissed her within one week. Stephen Braden and I proceeded to hammer out, point by point, a one-page contract. We faxed it to the hospitals and physicians, they signed, and we were in business!

Xantus was a success from the time we welcomed our first clients. The health care providers and our clients appreciated our sensitivity to their issues, and we grew by leaps and bounds. This reinforced my belief that you should surround yourself with positive people with a can-do attitude and remove those whose limitations are holding back your company. If they can't see the vision, lead them to the door.

TennCare proved every theory I had about managed care and competition. A free market radically changes the whole environment. As managed care organizations began furiously competing for new business, costs came under control. In its first five years, TennCare's reliance on the private managed care market saved the federal government $1.5 billion and eliminated what had always been known as the "Medicaid problem" in the state budget.

In the process, Tennesseans quickly grew to love TennCare. In 1998, a survey of five thousand TennCare households showed that satisfaction was greater than for members of commercial managed care programs.

At the same time, 93 percent of TennCare children saw a doctor regularly, compared with 85 percent under Medicaid. TennCare helped lower infant mortality rates, decrease the number of low-birth-weight babies, and reduce the number of teenage pregnancies. TennCare removed the welfare stigma of Medicaid and put the choices back in the hands of every consumer, regardless of income level. I guarantee that Medicaid never had TennCare's rate of success in improving people's health and lives.

While doing good, I was also doing very well. I have never worked so hard, been rewarded so well, and found it so satisfying. Xantus soon grew to be the third-largest managed care provider in the state. I made sure we enlisted the best hospitals and providers we could find.

We opened our offices on West End Avenue in Nashville. The company consisted of an almost equal number of black and white employees. We worked together well, and it felt more like a family than a cold, corporate environment. That doesn't mean, however, that I didn't expect a professional work ethic. I've never felt that strictness raises barriers; it raises expectations.

We addressed each other professionally, using "Mr.," "Mrs.," and "Miss" when appropriate. Punctuality is important—I'd usually get there first and make the coffee for everyone. When overtime was required to get something done, I didn't leave it to my staff. I stayed too, working alongside everyone else to make our deadline.

Unlike many CEOs, I outlawed "casual Friday." I believe it fosters a casual attitude about work that's all too common. If you're wearing your best-looking work clothes, you're going to feel your best, represent your company in the best way possible, and ultimately do a better job. I'm convinced of that.

Many budding entrepreneurs sought consultation from me. I never let that interfere with my time commitment to my company, but I devoted every Saturday to holding impromptu "clinics" for any young person just starting out in business. I got a tremendous sense of renewal from helping the next generation, especially young men and women of color. (For a distilled outline of what I shared with young entrepreneurs, see Howard's Law, pg. 147.)

One of the tips I offered was the "25 percent" rule. If you put in 25 percent more time at work, you're going to defeat your competition. Many of those young people are now success stories on their own. Kenneth Hardy of Bonnie Speed Delivery in Cleveland, Ohio, and Darryl Freeman of Zycron, an information technology service in Nashville, are two examples of that success.

I have always taken work seriously. Sometimes I find it difficult to understand why everyone doesn't share my dedication to it. Work has been my life, and I've loved it. I've wanted everyone to share in my excitement. I knew we were going to be a great success; and we were.

An entrepreneur is not a lonely island in the heart of the city. If you're going to get rich, someone else needs to get rich too. I had partners, although I always made sure I held the largest interest—essential, if you want to make good, timely decisions.

I have never prided myself on income, but on building net worth. Here's another suggestion for a budding entrepreneur: If you have an idea, make sure it's a big one. It takes as much work to make $100 thousand as it does to make $1 million.

I also found a level of acceptance in Nashville that I'd never dreamed possible. I dove into many civic activities, hungry to give something back to the community that had given me so much.

For years I'd given money to worthy causes such as Tennessee State University, the University of Tennessee, and Easter Seals. Then I began to give my time and expertise, serving as chairman of the Easter Seal Society of Tennessee, and chairman and director of the National Easter Seal Society.

I was also president and director of 100 Black Men of Middle Tennessee. My predecessors, Dr. T. B. Boyd III and Roland Jones, were both dynamic leaders, part of our original group of twenty-five who set out on a mission to enrich the lives of young, African American males. During my tenure as president, we were selected as 100 Black Men Chapter of the Year, also receiving national recognition from the Points of Light Foundation in Washington, D.C., and *USA Today Weekend* magazine.

Long before Bill Cosby created controversy by criticizing a black-youth culture that condemned education and correct speech as "acting white," I told the members of our group:

> The fabric of our community and our country can never reach its full potential if we continue to see the best opportunities for black boys as athletics or rap entertainment. . . . If they are smart enough to run gangs, they are smart enough to run corporations. If they have the marketing savvy to package and sell drugs, they can do the same for your product or mine.

In the last few years, I have received a lot of recognition for my work. In 1994, the Nashville NAACP branch gave me their Image Award for Lifetime Achievement. That same year, I received the National Conference of Christians and Jews Human Relations Award. The *Nashville Business Journal* named me their Small Business Executive of the Year in 1995. I was chosen in 1997 as Outstanding CEO among the one hundred largest privately held businesses in Nashville.

In 1997, the National Society of Fundraising Executives named me Philanthropist of the Year. My tears during the ceremony surprised even me, and my prayer before the crowd was simply this: "Dear Lord, make me worthy. Amen."

"A Better Sense of Who I Want to Ultimately Be"

Sam and I met through his work with Easter Seals. Of the thousands of people I have met in my life, Sam Howard's influence ranks in the top two. He brings out strength in people that they otherwise may have never known they had, or perhaps lost somewhere along the way, just living life.

He has a calmness about himself that comes from an unwavering faith. This calmness is reassuring to people who look to Sam for answers. That is very empowering. When he is in my presence, his mind is always going one hundred miles per hour. Ninety-nine percent of that time, it is going in a direction that is to help, encourage, or motivate another person. After having been in his presence, I always leave with a better sense of who I want to ultimately be.

—*Beverly Jones, court reporter and plaintiff for disabled court reporters' rights*

In 1998, I was named Nashvillian of the Year by the Easter Seal Society of Tennessee. In that same year, House Speaker Newt Gingrich appointed me to the National Bipartisan Commission on Medicare. The United States was beginning to seek answers to its nationwide problems of health care.

I received two wonderful honors in 1999: I was elected chairman of Nashville's Chamber of Commerce and I became a member of Oklahoma State University's Hall of Fame. Becoming chairman of the Chamber of Commerce was a unique accolade, speaking volumes about the acceptance I'd found in Nashville—I was the first person of color to be elected to the post. My tenure marked a number of accomplishments for the city's business community as the Chamber of Commerce:

- announced Dell Computers' manufacturing site;
- completed a transportation study to establish a rail line from Nashville to Lebanon;
- established the North Nashville Community Development Corporation;
- aided settlement of Nashville's public schools desegregation lawsuit;
- created a regional leadership institute at Middle Tennessee State University; and
- helped bring a professional football team, the Titans, to Nashville (who went to the Super Bowl in their first year).

I was deeply proud of everything we did at the Chamber of Commerce. Returning to OSU to see my former mentor, Dean Swearingen, however, and to hear him induct me into their business school's Hall of Fame, touched my heart deeply. Before they could see any of these accomplishments, my parents had died. I wish they could have seen and shared the fruits of my achievements. Their kid who loved

100 Black Men of Middle Tennessee

S ince 1991, this nonprofit group has dedicated itself to improving the future for African American boys in central Tennessee. The thirteenth affiliate of 100 Black Men of America Inc., the organization focuses on academic and social growth, preparing young black males for leadership roles.

The 100 Black Men organization has worked to counter the negative statistics of low literacy, poor academic performance, and low self-esteem often associated with black boys. The statistics for this group say it all:

- Leading Cause of Death: homicide
- High School Graduation Rate: 65 percent
- College Graduation Rate: 10 percent
- Poverty Rate (at or below): 40 percent
- Single Parent Household: 50 percent
- Newborn's Chance of Going to Prison: 1 in 4

The organization's plan for these young men's lives centers on the "4 Es": Education, Exposure, Experience, and Encouragement. By focusing specifically on young black males, the group seeks to galvanize the population as a whole. Milestones and initiatives include:

- A 1991 pledge to pay for college education for twenty-two male students at Ross Elementary, who are scheduled to graduate from high school in 2007. The group, called the "007," was selected as a whole, without academic or behavioral criteria.
- By 2004, scholarships totaling $216,000 were awarded for 2003–04 through an endowment funded solely by membership dues collected since 1991.
- More than 150 male students participate in programs offered in forty-five middle schools and universities.

- Core initiatives such as our 100 Kings project have shown dramatic improvement in test scores and positive behavior ratings. At the end of the first summer of this program, participants posted a 6 percent increase in vocabulary scores, 16 percent in reading, 5 percent in math, and 14 percent in mathematical story problems.
- The organization's focus on the holistic lives of boys also includes their parents, who are eligible for financial literacy and parenting skills programs.

—Samuel H. Howard

nice Schwinn bikes and had started a paper route to buy one was now driving a Jaguar. That's what I love about America and about American business. Anyone can do it, if you work hard enough and put yourself in God's hands.

I don't spend much time talking about the problems African Americans face when doing business. That's not because I don't think problems exist; it's because I choose not to focus on them. My father taught us to never focus on anything we couldn't change.

If I make a business proposal to someone and he turns it down, it may be because I'm black. Who knows? Who cares? I can do nothing about my skin color. I can, however, control the business proposition. I'm going to ask that person why he turned it down, and I'm going to try to come back with something better.

I've never been a believer in the politics of advocacy because of the law of unintended consequences of good intentions. They ultimately end up hurting the very people they're supposed to help.

It's human nature to act out of self-interest. I'm always suspicious when someone, such as a lawyer, says he's working on behalf of the poor or the downtrodden when he files a suit. I believe our welfare system trapped and enslaved a whole generation of people, particularly black people, while claiming to be compassionate. I believe that the people who are still defending entitlements for the poor are most often protecting their own jobs.

It is my opinion that more handouts will only worsen the problem. Instead, we must place more emphasis on self-reliance in public programs, including an appreciation of the economic and social system in which we live.

Recent governmental initiatives to push people out of federal aid and into jobs have, for the most part, exceeded almost everyone's expectations. The transition, especially for single mothers, has been difficult, but the biggest successes are those who have broken cycles of dependency that have lasted for generations.

Society is changing, and the need for once-necessary programs like affirmative action is receding. The stigma associated with being hired under affirmative action now outweighs its benefits. Our society should be as free as possible of discrimination; no laws should favor any group or class.

A quota is just a number. It's also a cap. If TennCare had a mandatory set-aside of 10 percent, we would not have had three black-owned managed care firms participating in TennCare and providing care for more than 30 percent of the TennCare population.

In the past, I frequently spoke to groups on the subjects of discrimination and free enterprise. After all, I was living proof of the American dream. It all came about without special favors or handouts. Everything happened because I worked toward a goal and kept my faith in God.

I made a speech in 1997 in which I said race was quickly becoming a nonissue for young people—yet another sign that we're moving from a race-based society to a meritocracy.

However, competition with China, and a new global economy, will be major challenges. This proves more true every day.

In 1997, I received an offer to buy Xantus. The offer exceeded any dream I'd ever had for myself, my family, or the company. The buyers offered approximately forty million dollars for the company that I'd founded for one million.

And yet . . . as I considered the offer, I also contemplated what I would lose if I accepted. I was fifty-eight, and I'd always dreamed of being CEO of a Fortune 500 company. I would never be hired to head one at my age.

My dream, like so many others before it, was beginning to take solid shape. I turned down the offer and prepared to fly to greater heights.

CHAPTER 7

PRISON WITHOUT BARS

In the LORD I take refuge; how can you say to me, "Flee like a bird to the mountains; for lo, the wicked bend the bow, they have fitted their arrow to the string, to shoot in the dark at the upright in heart; if the foundations are destroyed, what can the righteous do"?

—Psalm 11:1–3 (RSV)

*B*y now you have some idea of who I am and of how much I believe in this great country. I came from a little town in Oklahoma, and I grew up chopping peanuts during a time when my people were never expected to do anything more with their lives than that.

The dream of a better life for future generations was enough to sustain my father and mother through decades of menial labor. I never once heard them complain. Their dignity and valor were greater than I can express. I only wish they could have seen the successes I was able to attain, and the world in which their grandchildren, Buddy and Anica, have begun their careers.

The flight of the phoenix could have taken place only in America. I believe our country is the light of the world. Our free enterprise system and democratic society provide checks and balances that are the envy of every emerging nation.

101

Still, we have our problems. Among the greatest is the inability to provide adequate health care coverage to forty-four million uninsured individuals—this, in a country renowned for its medical prowess and technology.

As CEO of Xantus, I was doing well by doing good. With the TennCare program, we were providing health care to the state's uninsured. It was at the zenith of our success that I received the offer of close to forty million dollars for the company. Convinced that I could soar to even greater heights, I turned down the offer. I began to publicly state my intention of taking Xantus into the Fortune 500, expanded the business into Mississippi, and acquired a struggling TennCare MCO called HealthNet. In both the Nashville community and the nation-at-large, I was actively involved in leadership roles with many organizations, including the Nashville Chamber of Commerce (chairman-elect and chairman, 1997–99), National Bipartisan Commission on Medicare (1998), Mayor Bredesen's Crime Commission of 12, and 100 Black Men of Middle Tennessee (chairman 1997–99). Participating in these community activities and operating a three-hundred-million-dollar company was quite challenging without the benefit of a chief operating officer.

This may have been the turning point that led to my downfall. I still believed in our mission, but dreams of personal achievements brought about by my corporate success clouded my vision.

The Greeks called it "hubris": that fatal flaw of pride that precedes a downfall from a great height. Instead of continuing to focus on doing good, I concentrated on the dreams I'd long held for myself. I worked on expanding the company and being visibly active in Nashville and Washington, while at the same time aggressively lobbying the state to pay more attention to its crumbling TennCare system.

I question whether or not I might have been guilty of King Nebuchadnezzar's fallacy when, as the Bible relates, "as he looked out across the city, he said, 'Just look at this great city of Babylon! I, by my own mighty power, have built this beautiful city as my royal residence and as an expression of my royal splendor.'" As he was proudly boasting, he lost his kingdom.

Pride obscured what was clearly in front of me: For years, the state had failed to come through on its contractually agreed-upon rates of TennCare funding. The longer we

"They Forced Us to Pay for It"

The people who initiated TennCare didn't realize how complex it would be. They didn't think about the providers, or include them in the rule making at all. They felt they could underfund it and people could still get health care because some providers would still provide it. They forced community groups to provide care for those who had insurance but were unable to get their insurance to pay for that care. They forced us to pay for it. That was bad enough, but then they did not apply the rules equally to all companies. It affected Sam more than his share, because BlueCross was permitted to stop accepting uninsurables, but Xantus was not.

Health care is going to require a larger community of users to be successful. If you have a system where an insurance company can pick the best, the working middle class, and not include the poor and sick—if you can exclude all those and require TennCare to take them—it's hard to imagine how it will work. There has to be one insurable community, a national insurance program, like Medicare, for all people over age sixty-five. One community, so that [insurance companies] can't cherry pick.

—*Dr. Lloyd Elam, former president,*
Meharry Medical College

waited for the state to fulfill its contract, the more quickly TennCare was crumbling.

My decision to take on HealthNet hastened Xantus's end. But we could have easily survived that stress if the state had lived up to its agreements. And underfunding isn't the only issue the state has to answer for. As so often happens, a bureaucracy created to protect the public ended up using its powers to protect itself. With hawkeye retrospect, I can see the main issues that led to Xantus's—and TennCare's—downfall.

TennCare was a free-market experiment that might have become a pilot program for saving our national health care crisis. (In fact, at its birth, it was believed that TennCare might dovetail neatly with the Clinton administration's plan to come up with a national health care program.) However, once TennCare devolved from a capitalistic enterprise to a state-run agency, it lost its self-correcting aspect: the market-place. When functionaries and self-appointed advocates, rather than businesspeople and customers, started calling the shots, TennCare began to exhibit the worst excesses of Communism: Under the guise of helping the poor—and all people equally—TennCare really only helped the people who had the right political connections.

TennCare mightily rewarded those folks, politically and also monetarily, in the tens of millions of dollars, and with plum jobs. Behind closed doors, those in power rewarded their friends by alleviating some companies of risk, or bailing them out of minimum net worth requirements, while overzealously (and illegally) interpreting net worth requirements for others. These dealings have only recently begun to come to light, as reporters have begun asking questions about back-door deals directing taxpayer money to TennCare officials, including a former state senator who resigned after a federal bribery sting operation.

Like Politburo fat cats, TennCare's bureaucrats became expert at finding scapegoats for their own flaws, as well as maintaining the system that kept them in power. When TennCare's defects were becoming dangerously evident, bureaucrats found a way to place the blame on MCOs' management. Interestingly, accusations of financial malfeasance focused on managed care CEOs whose skin color matched mine.

In the meantime, our state bled red ink, our citizens lost their coverage, and I lost my good name. For a time, it looked like I might even go to jail. That's apparently no longer a danger, despite the state's efforts to make vague charges like "breach of fiduciary obligation" stick. My life is an open book—and so are my financial records. Even after the Tennessee Bureau of Investigation cleared me from the criminal investigation, and lawyers for the state made repeated efforts to settle their civil case against me, I was committed to fighting my enemies in court until completely vindicated. Isaiah 54:17 states: "No weapon formed against you shall prosper. And every tongue which rises against you in judgment, you shall condemn. This is the heritage of the servants of the LORD. And their righteousness is from Me, says the LORD" (NKJV).

Assess the Political Risk

What happened to Sam's company was really a matter of politics. You can see it today in mutual funds or insurance. Or health care. When there is a political advantage, politicians will use it to get votes. It's not a matter of right or wrong. It's a matter of getting votes. On the other side, you have people who have no risk, but every advantage to attack. You need to assess if you will be at risk. No one teaches you about that political risk you take.

—*Mike Walker, entrepreneur*

I offer this chapter as explanation for what happened to my company—and to TennCare. What happened to me or to those who have lost their health care coverage, isn't even the worst of it: By focusing on destroying whistle-blowers such as myself, instead of fixing TennCare's faults, these bureaucrats have snuffed out the best chance for a free-market-based national health care plan that could really work.

Xantus's main problems were both simple and complex. Some of them were mere oversights that cost the company dearly; others were, in hindsight, ill-timed business decisions. But we would have survived all of that, if not for the major flaws in TennCare which were compounded by its bureaucrats' campaign to thwart a potentially major lawsuit by a whistleblower—me.

Xantus: A Company's Fiery Descent

1. Underfunding

The annual multimillion-dollar profits of Xantus from 1994–96 were reversed with losses of nearly $16 million in '97 and $40 million in '98. In March of '99, when I took the company into rehabilitation, it was insolvent. Why?

A detailed report, prepared with the help of my lawyers and professional auditors, shows how adverse political decisions compounded the state's failure to fulfill its financial agreement to its MCOs. By our figures, if the state had met its contractual obligation to fund TennCare and had not changed rules midstream (allowing retroactive enrollment and new transplant patients), Xantus would have earned profits of $2.5 million in '97 and close to $10 million in '98.

Instead, our operations deteriorated. The company's crisis was exactly what I'd predicted in that 1993 letter to Health and Human Services Chief Donna Shalala, in which I'd detailed the inadequacy of TennCare's funding and attached an analysis by my accounting firm. The numbers simply did not add up. In essence, by not funding TennCare as promised, the state was asking MCOs to fund its portion out of our pockets.

In March 1999, another respected accounting firm, PricewaterhouseCoopers (PwC), independently corroborated my statements in a report prepared for the Tennessee comptroller ("Actuarial Review of Capitation Rates in the TennCare Program"). With so many MCOs in trouble, the state finally took a long, hard look at its numbers. PwC concluded that "the methods used to develop capitation rates for TennCare are not consistent with generally accepted standards." After detailing the inconsistencies, the auditors concluded that MCOs should have received sixteen dollars more per member per month in order to be actuarially sound.

If the state had paid those rates as promised, Xantus would have increased its revenues by $15.2 million in '97 and $33.8 million in '98. (I'm glad to say that after the PwC report, the state finally increased its TennCare funding, which rescued other failing MCOs.)

In the chart that follows, you'll see just how much money the state actually lost in the long run by initially underfunding TennCare. Finally, in 1999, the increase kicked in, but by that time TennCare consumed increasingly higher percentages of the state's budget, as uninsurables soared.

When the state ignored Xantus's requests to correct this underfunding, we announced our intentions to pursue a seventy-five-million-dollar lawsuit to force the state to abide by its contract if it would not do so voluntarily. This announcement brought about a string of political repercussions, beginning with the resignation of one high-profile Xantus board member credited with instituting TennCare. Against my better judgment, I eventually decided against filing the lawsuit, believing that in business, a lawsuit should

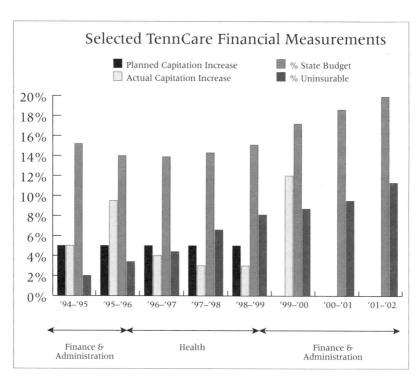

Planned versus actual capitation increases, percent of the state budget, and growth in number of uninsurables covered under TennCare while TennCare was under the direction of the State Department of Finance and Administration, and under the State Department of Health.

be the last resort. I took my lawyers' advice and voluntarily placed Xantus into rehabilitation, hoping that their predictions of a better working environment for correcting its problems would pan out.

However, my threatened lawsuit had another effect: It drew a circle of TennCare bureaucrats into action against me. The fact that I didn't go through with the lawsuit only made me more vulnerable.

2. Retroactive Enrollments

Other factors made our situation worse. In 1996, the state allowed BlueCross/BlueShield, which was its largest insurer and critical to the success of the TennCare program, to close its TennCare enrollment. As every insurer knows, the competitive playing field is level only if risk is shared equally among all insurers. Xantus and other managed care companies were now forced to take on uninsurables which would have gone to BlueCross. Retroactive enrollments, for which Xantus sometimes received a bill months or years after treatment, cost Xantus $5.5 million in '97 and $7.6 million in '98. As Senator Douglas Henry later wrote, such retroactive payments were "contrary to the principle of insurance, which is that you cannot insure against a loss which has already occurred."

We also began to find that private insurers were denying coverage to their patients needing transplants, in effect sending the transplant patients to TennCare. After three months in TennCare, a patient would have the transplant, at a cost of $35,000 or more. If these clients had been distributed fairly among all companies, we would not have had a problem, but assigning whole pools to Xantus weighted us down mightily. We asked to close our enrollment as Blue Cross did, but were denied that privilege by the state.

I warned the state once again. In a 1997 letter to the Bureau of TennCare, I described the problems of uninsurables and retroactive enrollments as "fundamental problems which, if not timely corrected . . . could cause the TennCare program to fail." These problems continue to plague TennCare HMOs.

I still don't know why the state allowed BlueCross/ BlueShield to close its enrollment, then proceeded to assign TennCare uninsurables to the other MCOs, particularly Xantus. Perhaps the state feared its biggest MCO would go under. But forcing the rest of the state's MCOs to take on a greater proportional risk was not good business. In fact, it smacked of politics.

The state had established an "adverse selection" fund to help redress costs to MCOs who had taken on unusually high numbers of very sick TennCare enrollees. But as Xantus scrambled to survive its financial crisis, TennCare paid it nothing from the adverse selection fund between July 1997 and December 1998. The state administrators' explanation for this was that they were working on a formula to determine how the funds would be distributed.

When the state finally came up with one, it ignored the recommendation of its own actuary, focusing instead on a more politically acceptable course of action by favoring BlueCross, whose participation was required for TennCare to continue. BlueCross ended up with 50 percent of funds in the adverse selection pool, even though their enrollment had been closed! The Bureau of TennCare's own adverse selection data for the period of July 1997 through December 31, 1998 (the period in which BlueCross closed enrollment) indicates that Xantus Healthplan and Access MedPlus received adverse selection reimbursements of 6.0 percent and 6.5 percent, respectively, of the Bureau's estimated adverse selection costs of their members. Programwide, MCOs received 17.9 percent reimbursements from these funds, Vanderbilt Healthplan received 61.5 percent, and Memphis TLC received 59.2 percent.

3. Micromanagement and Consent Decrees Under the Department of Health

The business climate cooled further in 1997, when TennCare oversight moved from the State Department of Finance and Administration to the State Department of Health. The Department of Finance dealt regularly with businesses and understood the basics of a profit system. Profits are, after all, the engine that drives MCOs to invest in TennCare.

Before the move, Xantus and other MCOs were allowed autonomy in managing the care of their enrollees. The state's hands-off approach under the Department of Finance changed to micromanagement under the Department of Health. Enrollee satisfaction under TennCare was naturally important to state officials, but there was no interest in ensuring a decent rate of return to TennCare's MCOs.

In addition to taking on uninsurables, we were also ordered to cover services that we'd never covered before and without any corresponding increase in compensation, which meant additional costs of $1.1 million in '97 and $5.7 million in '98.

Under the Department of Health, the state steadily increased its powers over the operations of Xantus and other MCOs, using its monopoly position to make the company little more than another state agency. Advocacy lawyers, paid by the state, spearheaded this thrust by winning court orders based on anecdotal client information and their zest for "doing good" no matter what it cost. Once acting on behalf of "the poor" under Medicaid, these advocacy lawyers now acted on behalf of a greatly increased constituency under TennCare, which treated the poor plus the uninsured. Eight hundred thousand Tennesseans had qualified for Medicaid; up to 1.2 million Tennesseans, about one-fourth of the state's population, qualified for TennCare.

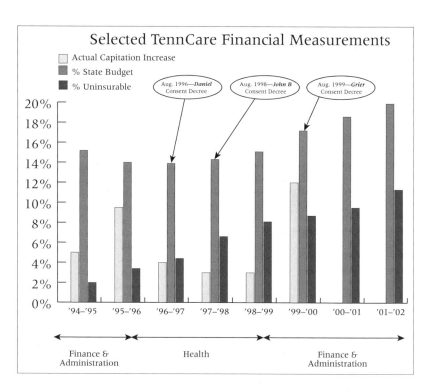

Consent Decrees' Impact on State Budget and Uninsurables while TennCare was under the direction of the State Department of Finance and Administration and under the State Department of Health.

Bottom Line

As an experiment in the use of the free market to provide health benefits, TennCare is essentially dead. In its place are the TennCare consent decrees, solutions created by lawyers. Daniels resolved coverage disputes through litigation. John B. reintroduced Medicaid law and policy for enrollees under the age of 21. Grier abolished coverage limits for all other enrollees. What is left of TennCare is the contracting out of some government services to HMOs. Otherwise, TennCare is little more than the old Medicaid program, but with more beneficiaries and benefits than when the state resorted to market solutions because of budget pressures. Worse, the state has given up control over TennCare by its concessions, shutting out the General Assembly and leaving it in the hands of a few self-appointed representatives of the TennCare enrollees.

—Mark Chen, attorney-at-law

Several changes in eligibility requirements chipped away at TennCare's effectiveness, but three consent decrees were crucial blows. One changed Early and Periodic Screening, Diagnosis and Treatment (EPSDT) requirements, ordering TennCare HMOs to keep track of enrollees' appointments and provide transportation and scheduling assistance—tasks normally expected of social workers. Benefits expanded to include "maintenance services which prevent or mitigate the worsening of conditions or prevent the development of additional health problems." There were no lifetime dollar amounts or absolute service limits set for children under the age of twenty-one.

At the time, I had faith that these bureaucratic anomalies would eventually correct themselves. The state would discover that the MCOs' financial viability was as important

as enrollee satisfaction, and that Xantus was healthy enough
to ride out a pretty rough storm until it did. We had made a
profit in the years from 1994 through 1996 and had not paid
any dividends. Yet we had to invest another $7.1 million in
the Healthplan in 1997 and 1998.

The chart on page 112 shows how the critical consent
decrees correspond to the steady rise in TennCare's percentage
of the state budget, as well as creeping rates of uninsurables.

4. HealthNet Acquisition

In May of 1997, after I sold my radio station, I saw my
chance to expand Xantus. As any businessperson knows,
hard times also create opportunities. Risk is usually
involved, but that's how "buy low, sell high" works. I
bought another struggling HMO, HealthNet, operated by
Baptist Hospital. I believed that with greater economies of
scale, we could offer even better service to our enrollees. In
addition to the boost in total assets from HealthNet into
Xantus Corporation, the MCO's acquisition put another $5
million into Xantus Healthplan's net worth.

Unfortunately, however, HealthNet also brought us
unforeseen difficulties: My biggest mistake was assuming
the liabilities for processing their backlog of one hundred
thousand reported claims and their IBNR (incurred but not
reported) claims.

Those claims required us to establish a second claims
payment system until we could incorporate HealthNet into
our own computer system. The many snafus resulting from
this second payment system marked the beginning of our
significant decline in reputation.

Now, of course, I believe my push to expand the company
and advance my career is what led to my downfall. In retrospect, it wasn't necessary or prudent to take on greater risk in
TennCare's shaky environment. I think God had a better plan
for my success, even though I had already set my own flight

plan. I want to emphasize, however, that my mistakes were lapses in business judgment. I never—never—did anything improper, much less illegal.

5. Statutory Net Worth Requirement

At the same time that Xantus was bleeding red ink, the Department of Commerce and Insurance successfully lobbied the state legislature to increase the statutory net worth requirements for MCOs operating in Tennessee. This legislation, enacted in 1997, was yet another indication of the state's push to force MCOs to fund TennCare for the state. As of January 1, 1998, Xantus Healthplan had a statutory reserve requirement of $1,185,000. But on January 1, 1998, the company's statutory reserve requirement leaped sevenfold, to $7,043,344. The Department of Commerce and Insurance had arrived at this inflated reserve requirement for Xantus by adding into our annual revenue statement the revenues of our newly acquired MCO, HealthNet, for eleven months before it was acquired.

This methodology was clearly contradictory to the state law that outlined the rules for establishing net worth requirements. But it was the first shot in a pattern of harassment that began one month after the merger. Suddenly, the Commerce and Insurance Department's minimum net worth requirements for TennCare MCOs, made more stringent in 1998, came under the harshest scrutiny we'd experienced, and the dispute over the minimum net worth continued throughout 1998.

My lawyer's review of the Commerce and Insurance Department's public files found that the Bureau of TennCare apparently decided to follow the department's lead in aggressively regulating Xantus Healthplan. He wrote in a report:

> When the extent of the unpaid claims at HealthNet became known, politics probably kept [the Bureau of TennCare] from backing off their regulatory efforts. The

Bureau's insistence on weekly supervision and a prompt
resolution of the claims backlog increased Xantus' financial problems. The Bureau's apparent search for reasons to
retain the withhold [i.e., continue withholding contractually agreed-upon payments] made matters worse.
HealthNet's problems made it likely that Xantus
Healthplan, unless it received a large infusion of capital,
would need time to integrate the merger. Instead, the
Commerce Department refused to give Xantus any
leeway, while giving the other HMOs almost every
favorable interpretation of the law that was possible.
With respect to Xantus, the Department of Commerce
appears to have thought that it could force the company
into getting additional capital and, when it did not
succeed, considered receivership inevitable or else did
not care if that was the final result.

Examples of this bureaucratic leeway were also uncovered
in public files. The Commerce and Insurance Department
allowed one MCO to delay its review of 1997 quarterly statements until that MCO could receive its adverse selection
payment and correct its net worth deficiencies for that year.
This MCO, which was significantly smaller than Xantus
Healthplan, received over $5.3 million. That's $1.8 million
more than the plan had expected to receive in adverse selection receipts. With this payment, the MCO met its statutory
net worth requirement.
My lawyer wrote:

> It appears that the statute and the TennCare Contract gave
> the Commerce and Insurance Department a great deal of
> latitude in regulating the TennCare HMOs. By using this
> latitude, the Commerce and Insurance Department
> appears to have avoided regulating or enforcing net worth
> requirements [on that TennCare MCO for over a year].

In another MCO's case, the Commerce and Insurance
Department "appears to have accepted the unilateral reduc-
tion of its claims" liability to satisfy a net worth requirement.

"In effect," my lawyer wrote, "the Commerce Department can decide when it will apply the law to a TennCare MCO."

6. Partner Company's Computer Errors

In January 1998, as we strained to cope with rapidly increasing enrollment and demand for services, our pharmacy benefit manager, MIM Health Plan Inc., implemented a new computer system to track pharmacy orders—a new system that erroneously neglected to include enrollees' required seven-dollar copayment. This error, which went undetected until January 1999, cost Xantus eight million dollars in 1998.

Clearly, it was our fault for not detecting this oversight earlier. In May of 1998, I asked our staff to review the skyrocketing pharmacy costs. They looked at traditional causes such as use and cost of specific drugs but neglected to talk to our partner to see whether they had made any administrative changes. A nurse found the error in January of 1999 when I asked her to find the reasons for the pharmacy cost increases.

Although MIM immediately agreed to extend Xantus $2.5 million in credit against invoices once the oversight was uncovered, the damage had been done.

We had severe problems bringing HealthNet's claims into our information processing system. Because our systems were incompatible, we were forced to duplicate HealthNet's system until we could bring them into ours. Replicating HealthNet's system proved to be unwieldy, slow, and complex. It took Xantus months to sort out the problems. We were known for paying our physicians and providers promptly, at among the highest rates in the industry. As we tried to sort through our inherited HealthNet backlog of one hundred thousand claims, however, our ordinarily happy physicians and hospital providers began to complain about delayed payments.

Xantus intended to provide excellent service. After all, we weren't dealing with a commodity, but people's health. In the fall of 1998, I asked KPMG to audit the claims procedure, then we implemented their advice on how to improve it. Within one year, our claims accuracy had improved to 97 percent.

Such slow progress was not enough. We reeled under our losses.

7. Loss of Investment Capital/SunTrust/ Equitable Securities Engagement

Xantus Corporation, the MCO's parent company, held a $22.5 million credit line with NationsBank. Because of TennCare's refusal to allow Xantus Healthplan to close enrollment and stabilize its medical losses and TennCare underfunding, the bank refused to allow Xantus Corporation the use of its remaining credit to bolster reserves.

We took a proactive approach to this problem and sought strategic partners on our own initiative. Xantus Corporation engaged Equitable Securities on August 26, 1998, with the goal of finding private financing or a strategic partner by no later than December 31, 1998. We'd had a long, strong relationship with Equitable, one of the best-known names in the securities business, since the inception of our company.

On September 24, 1998, James H. S. Cooper, managing director with SunTrust/Equitable Securities, reported to the Xantus Corporation board with his findings. He identified both state governmental regulations and general market conditions surrounding managed care at the time as potential limitations. Because of our long association, he said that SunTrust/Equitable Securities was very familiar with all the positive aspects of Xantus Corporation. Mr. Cooper pointed out that Xantus had been more generous to providers than most other plans. Further, his analysis of TennCare made him thoroughly conversant with the problems we'd regularly dealt with as a board—i.e., underfunding, retroactive enrollment, adverse selection, and micromanagement of the program. Ultimately, however, Mr. Cooper reported that Equitable was unable to find a partner or funding for Xantus.

In short, Equitable's search for a partner or funding was unsuccessful not because of our management, but because of concern about the TennCare sector of our business. TennCare's underfunding and inept management had become national knowledge in the investment community.

8. $87 Million Debt Fraud

After I voluntarily took Xantus into rehabilitation, the state-appointed rehabilitation team claimed our company owed $87 million of debt to providers, a figure that was subsequently reported throughout the media. When I analyzed this report, however, I found the rehabilitators had overstated the actual amount of provider claims by $50 million. Two consultants, who'd formed their partnership expressly for the task of rehabilitating Xantus, had commissioned a questionable statistical claims study by a consulting firm called Navigant. That firm had counted spurious claims along with others, accounting for most of the overestimation. The balance of the inflated figure came from including claims that violated timely filing and rate provisions of the provider contracts with Xantus Healthplan.

9. Conflicts of Interest Among Rehabilitators

Xantus had announced the intention to pursue means to force the state to abide by its contract. Although I decided against filing a lawsuit against the state, my announcement had resulted in a string of political repercussions. At the advice of my lawyers, and with the hope of working out our problems with the fewest complications for our enrollees and employees, I voluntarily took Xantus into rehabilitation.

After I decided against filing the suit, I followed my lawyers' advice and began working with the state's rehabilitation plan. However, rather than appointing people specifically experienced in operating an HMO to bring Xantus back to fiscal health, the state appointed two former TennCare chief administrators, who'd helped invent the program. They even formed a consulting firm for the express purpose of rehabilitating Xantus. And they weren't the only two involved in the rehabilitation process who had direct links to administering TennCare. Several members of the rehabilitation team's lawyers and consultants had former ties to the Health Department (including two former commissioners) and other aspects of the program.

TennCare had been one of Tennessee's most popular public programs, but no one—certainly no bureaucrat or elected official—wanted to take the blame when their decisions to expand coverage and deny or delay payments created problems. In hindsight, the state's rehabilitation plan wasn't business as usual, or even business at all. This was politics. I should have pressed the state to fulfill its obligations.

We later learned that the two former TennCare administrators billed the state for thirty thousand dollars per month, *each*, for their consulting efforts.

At the time, I hoped we would at last have the state's cooperation in fixing our problems. I instructed our staff to cooperate with the rehabilitators' efforts, and we got used to seeing them in our offices every day.

In the beginning, the consultants offered me a quick exit from Xantus, no questions asked. In a meeting with my family, we unanimously agreed to fight. I didn't want to leave Xantus under a cloud of suspicion; I wanted to clear my name.

When the consultants took so long to come up with a restructuring plan that it looked like we might begin to lose doctors and hospitals, I drafted a rehabilitation plan myself. I then showed it to a former commissioner of finance and a former commissioner of insurance, and they offered several good suggestions that I incorporated into my nine-page plan. On the advice of some experienced state lobbyists who were personal friends, I couriered the plan all over town to decision makers such as government commissioners (including the rehabilitators' boss), key legislators, hospital providers, and physicians. The response was positive.

My quick and decisive actions to address the company's problems proved to be political missteps. I received a number of letters of endorsement from hospital creditors, but my end run had a negative impact on the rehabilitators' image. They were charging the state sixty thousand dollars a month to come up with a workable plan, and I'd beaten them to it.

The consultants strenuously objected to my submitting a rehabilitation plan and filed the first of two scathing reports attacking me. They wove a cocoon of innuendo, falsely reporting the company's operations, my salary, and the company's operating condition.

At long last they acted: First on their list of recommendations was that I resign from the company I had founded. Before long, someone hinted at a criminal investigation to the newspaper.

My family and I discussed the alternatives. I could fight the rehabilitators, which could cost me every cent I had and might take years. In the meantime, Xantus Healthplan would be destroyed and our employees driven out. The trust with clients and physicians that we'd built up over the years was already eroding.

If I stepped down, our clients would be assured continued health care and my employees would keep their jobs. Our providers, many of whom had been waiting for months after the state cut off our payments, would be paid. I was confident that state administrators would eventually determine the true root of the company's problems. I was confident enough of my financial management and staff to leave the records of Xantus as an open book in front of anyone who wanted to look at them.

Besides, even if I stepped down, I could still fight to clear my name. My legal and political advisers urged me to take this course. They believed that my stepping down as Xantus Healthplan's CEO would represent a cooperative relationship with the state, which would be the best atmosphere for working out both my own legal problems and those of Xantus. We believed that if I backed down from my confrontational pose, the state would do so as well, and that we'd all work this out without further threat of suits or criminal charges. My family and I agreed it was time for me to remove myself from the management of Xantus Healthplan.

I took Xantus Healthplan's parent, Xantus Corporation, and moved to Brentwood. My assistant, Tanya Hausmann, decided to come with me to pursue new opportunities, and my son, Buddy, came along as well. Most of my old Xantus hires were offered jobs with the rehabilitators. I had confidence that the people I'd hired, who'd done their jobs well, would be able to tell the rehabilitators what had happened.

Despite our differences, I believed the two consultants, as former TennCare administrators, would be able to find out what was wrong and fix it. I believed they had the intellectual curiosity to get to the bottom of the state's TennCare crisis. I believed that no matter what their preconceived notions were, that once they looked at the numbers, they would have to face the facts as I had found them: The state had underfunded and overmanaged TennCare.

I was wrong.

My former employees tell me that the rehabilitators entered our offices convinced that I had taken money from the state, and they were determined to find it. Apparently, they never strayed from that prejudicial notion—perhaps because finding otherwise would mean admitting that TennCare, their brainchild, was less than perfect.

Some of my former employees continued to work with Xantus, but the senior management, financial, and information technology people almost immediately began to look for other jobs. They later told me the atmosphere was so hostile that they could not continue there. They said that they told the rehabilitators what had really happened, but the rehabilitators simply wouldn't be shaken from proving their agenda—that I'd taken money from the state.

One of the consultants later confirmed his bias in a court statement: "When I walked in the door [at Xantus], [the other consultant] and I . . . had the potential of the entire TennCare program, which we helped create, very honestly, and have a great deal of closeness to, going down the tube." The two were willing to protect that program's image at all costs. I openly agreed from the start that the HealthNet acquisition strained Xantus; we had problems we were working to correct. But never once, in the years since independent auditors KPMG confirmed my analysis of underfunding and unsound actuary rates, never once have these consultants admitted that TennCare's flaws might have adversely affected Xantus.

Instead of fixing Xantus, or TennCare, the rehabilitators essentially became prosecutors, charging me with criminal acts. At the same time, they absolved themselves—while making a handsome profit.

The consultants continued their investigation of the company and of me over the next year. They had twelve months to file charges against me. I was warned by politically savvy friends that after such a long investigation, the consultants could not very well walk away without charging me with something. On the very last day they could legally do so, the rehabilitators filed a civil suit, charging me with the theft of nine million dollars in state funds from Xantus.

Every effort I'd made to cooperate with the state had come to nothing.

At last there was a suit to flesh out that June 1999 innuendo of when someone leaked word that my company was under criminal investigation for "breach of fiduciary obligation" by the TBI.

In their derogatory report filed against Xantus management, the rehabilitators alleged that Xantus consistently failed to maintain the requried statutory capital; transferred TennCare funding to its parent company, Xantus Corporation, for unrelated purposes including a transfer of $9 million in May 1988; operated an ineffective provider claims processing system; lacked formality in accounting and management practices; and lacked experienced management.

The allegations took my breath away. Where did they think the money had gone? My own net worth had dropped dramatically over the last couple of years, some of it going directly into Xantus. I may be the only person in Tennessee who has put his own money into TennCare.

Xantus did prove to be quite profitable in its last years— for the rehabilitators. Between March 1999, when the two former TennCare administrators took charge of Xantus, and December 2004, rehabilitators' fees alone were $2 million. Adding in lawyers' and other consultants' fees for "rehabilitation" of Xantus, the total was $12.3 million. By 2005, long after Xantus had closed, the total rehabilitation costs had climbed to $59.4 million.

I've cooperated fully with the authorities. When no one from the TBI or any law enforcement agency contacted me about that highly publicized rumor of a criminal charge, I took the lead to clear my name. I asked my lawyers to contact an assistant district attorney to begin an investigation.

After years under a cloud of suspicion, I received a two-sentence letter stating that the U.S. attorney's office in Middle Tennessee had no basis to seek criminal charges against me, and no criminal charges would be sought.

Eventually, I decided I could no longer afford cooperation and patience in my efforts to seek justice. During the lawsuit, the state claimed that the management contract between Xantus and the Healthplan had been modified (and thus I wasn't entitled to compensation). The court ruled that the contract had not been modified. This led me to file a claim for unpaid management fees of $46 million and a modest amount of legal fees. This countersuit was an effort to force the state to recognize both its injustices against me and the real problems in TennCare.

I've witnessed a few interesting developments along the way: The judge in charge of the rehabilitation of Xantus expressed outrage at invoices submitted by the rehabilitators, initially refusing to pay them. After her decision was challenged, she appointed a special master to examine the invoices, who also took issue with these amounts. (On appeal, however, another judge ordered the invoices to be paid.)

The judge also wisely began asking questions about the consultants' rehabilitation plan for Xantus. The consultants assured her in 1999 that Xantus was "ready to turn the corner" toward profitability. A year later, the consultants tried—and failed—to find a buyer for Xantus (in part, I believe, to keep the judge from reverting the company to my control).

In 2003, Xantus closed. Its 125,000 remaining members were transferred to a special BlueCross/BlueShield emergency TennCare program.

Today, as the state tries to save its tattered TennCare program (and the lives of the people who depend on it), reporters continue to uncover evidence of government officials who enriched themselves through a program for the poor that they were charged with overseeing.

Meanwhile, my world has changed. My barless prison takes many forms. I have a nice house, but sometimes I can't help feeling like a caged bird. Sometimes my walled backyard no longer seems to exist to protect my privacy, but rather to hold me in. I often sit there, near a small fountain, and wonder how this could have happened. Not officially charged with any crime, yet in the court of public opinion, I was guilty until proven innocent.

I've found that my once-golden reputation now makes it difficult for me to raise money for new ventures. In one instance, I could not convince a longtime banking partner to provide funding with 100 percent equity. As any entrepreneur knows, capital is a deal's lifeblood.

My lawyers became the guards in my prison. The process ground slowly on, moved forward only by my legal team. State administrators did not halt their efforts against me—nor did they save Xantus, or TennCare.

I would have preferred to win this battle by helping to point out and correct TennCare's faulty management and shaky financial underpinnings—and by having my good name restored. In the long run, that's going to do everyone the most good—especially the state's uninsured.

I've been hopeful that a full investigation would illuminate TennCare's problems and that I would be absolved. I've been proved only partly right. TennCare funding was finally increased, but despite my efforts, the state has neither cleared my name nor has it indicted me. At this point, I don't know if my reputation can ever be salvaged.

I believe, sadly, that cases like mine happen quite often in our country. My story is complex, not easily explained in a paragraph or two of a newspaper story. Clouded in suspicion, my professional life hangs in the balance.

"The Deck Was Stacked"

When Sam came to me and told me what he was doing, it always worried me because I felt it would be difficult, if not impossible, to build a company that was viable as a freestanding institution. He was willing to take a risk. Many of us wanted him to succeed. And his company became quite large. I always felt that our state government did not provide him the proper support to see that this significant black-led enterprise had every possibility of succeeding. Instead they put barriers in the way. . . . I'm not sure managed care could possibly work in the state and provide enough margin to succeed. Sam and the team he put together were as good as anyone's, but the deck was stacked against him. However, Sam always conducted himself with great dignity. I never saw a lack of support for Sam and his family. It never hurt him or his effectiveness, either one.

—Dr. Thomas Frist, former CEO, HCA;
board chairman, Frist Foundation and many other entities

As I've said before, we learn the most from failure—and I've learned a lot. Understanding what happened at Xantus is probably the best business lesson I could teach. It's also a morality tale for any public figure who wishes to solve our health care crisis.

I believe that God also wants me to allow Him to do His work. I feel a responsibility to get my story out, as clearly as I can. Now I'm going to sit back and let Him do the rest. It's hard, but I'm trying to have faith.

After all, if His eye is on the sparrow, He must also watch the flight of a phoenix.

It is Finished! . . . (John 19:30 NKJV)

On November 20, 2006, the state of Tennessee agreed to dismiss with prejudice the $9 million lawsuit against me and settle my personal and corporate claims against the state. We received a significant cash settlement and the state dropped all its claims against us. With this settlement and dismissal, my frequent, incessant prayer of Psalm 26:1 ("Vindicate me, O LORD, For I have walked in my integrity" NKJV) had finally been realized after seven long years. In 2001, my brother Maurice told me on the day of my first court hearing that I was not to fear because of Isaiah 54:17. I wrote that New King James Scripture on a stick-up sheet and kept it in my checkbook up until just two days before the settlement. It reads:

> "No weapon formed against you shall prosper, And every tongue which rises against you in judgment You shall condemn. This is the heritage of the servants of the LORD, And their righteousness is from Me," Says the LORD.

Amen.

A WING
AND A PRAYER

Consider it pure joy, my brothers, whenever you face trials of many kinds, because you know that the testing of your faith develops perseverance.

—James 1:2–3 (NIV)

*D*espite my own success, I realize that progress still comes too slowly for minority businesspeople. In a 2005 speech to the Urban League, I noted that the authors of the U.S. Constitution counted enslaved African Americans as three-fifths, or 60 percent, of a white person. According to the 2004 Equality Index, the African Americans' status is still just 73 percent of the economic condition of whites. However, many things have changed for the better. In that same speech, I noted that when Karan and I first arrived in Nashville, we were a lonely island and each other's only confidante. Black businesspeople could have held meetings in a phone booth. Then I introduced the young minority businesspeople at the meeting and asked them to stand, one by one. It was a long list; soon there were many standing all over the room. Some had come to me over the years for advice and had become great successes on their own. It was a proud moment for all of us.

My entrepreneurial efforts are as successful as ever, and my friends and business associates are solidly supportive. But perhaps the most satisfying work I've done is helping along others who want to follow my flight pattern.

I've had so many great mentors, and I learned much from them. I'm glad I've also been able to help a few others along the way.

Like me, they've learned that success is not an entitlement. It comes from hard work, impeccable integrity, equal opportunity, and divine consequences in a capitalistic system.

I asked a few of my mentees to share their stories with you to demonstrate not only business success, but human success. They illustrate one lesson that business school case histories can't teach: You have to let the phoenix fly.

Anthony Tate
CEO, Tate Commercial Services
Nashville

I graduated with a history degree from Middle Tennessee State University in '93. When I was about to graduate, I realized I loved business. I did everything—threw parties, had a greeting card business, a groundskeeping business, and did Web design. A true entrepreneur is someone who doesn't give up.

I had a full-time job and a second job, too. Then I sort of broke down; I was worn out. I quit and took a temp job. It didn't take long to realize I didn't really want to do that. Then I ran into a couple of Phi Beta Sigma brothers who were each in charge of cleaning a bank. One of them let me tag along to learn the business.

The first client I got was a guy who owned just one building. I had approached him correctly, with a brochure. I started cleaning his building and was able to get out from under that hourly job.

I later saw an ad for an assistant manager to clean at BellSouth. The BellSouth tower is the tallest in Nashville. I went there and met Mark Isom of Premier Building Maintenance. He was my age, about thirty-five. I thought it was fantastic that a black man was in charge of cleaning the tallest building in the city. He hired me and I outworked everybody there.

I also worked for some other companies, cleaning the American Building, Meharry Medical College, Dreamworks Studio, and Vanderbilt. I had sixty-five employees, and the highest scores from customers. I now knew how to clean large-scale buildings. I jumped out on faith, actually leaving a fifty-thousand-dollar-a-year job to clean three banks on my own.

I started out with a pretty big contract, but I knew I was going to need some help. The Nashville Business Incubation

Center helped me. I started going to Sam's open meetings every fourth Monday at downtown TSU because I had been hearing Sam's name for a long time. I arrived there real early, hoping I might get some extra time with him. The first thing this guy says to me is, "You're going to be one of the big guys in this business if you keep doing what you're doing and be patient."

He was right. I'm a janitor, so the job isn't very glamorous, but now we have a half-million dollar business with twenty-three employees. It's great to have someone like Sam give feedback. It's great just to be in the business community.

As you go out and get business, Sam puts you in front of decision makers. He'll say, call this woman at the Urban League. I told her you were going to call. He'll tell her, "I've got this young guy, he's very good." You can imagine how good that feels. He's a great encourager. He says, "Just continue to do what you're doing."

I come from the 'hood, and my mom is still my biggest influence. My father was an alcoholic, and I had a rough coming up. But my mom has a real strong religious background and she helped me know that I could do anything. I always knew I was going to go to college, even as early as third or fourth grade. We still talk every day. I always talked about my thoughts. She'd say, "It's good to have those thoughts, but not if you don't do anything about them." Because of her, I have the utmost respect for women and elderly people. I just listen to people, those who have done what I want to do, and I just do what they did.

I'm trying to be just like Sam, but I try not to call him too much. I think people used to be scared to help other people. We need to be sure our black men and women are working. If there were more Sam Howards, African American business would be way high on the food chain. He has the humblest attitude. All these guys have the same type of nature. They don't have to be scared of sharing. God or someone has something for me to do. I'm going to try to be a good citizen and improve. Sam says just pass it on.

Darrell Freeman
CEO, Zycron
Chairman, Nashville Chamber of Commerce, 2006–2007
Nashville

I graduated from MTSU. I've been working on my own for thirteen years, after one year with a company, Sting Ray Computer Services, as a computer engineer.

In 1991 I started Zycron, wanting to do computer sales and computer services. We had mostly computer sales at that time. With the Internet, I saw computers becoming a commodity and knew there would be fierce competition if everybody went online to see what everybody else's prices were, so I started to focus on the service aspect as far as information technology (IT) staffing and outsourcing.

There's been a big demand for it, has been for the last four or five years. Last year there was a low in the industry, but it was a record year for us. I think it was persistence, determination, good relationships, and a diverse client base. We currently employee about 145 people and we are hiring twenty more this month.

We've had steady growth every year and expect to grow about 20 percent this year. I'm focused on growing at the right pace. The first several years, I didn't really know what was I was doing; I was just trying to make a living. Now we are focused on steady growth. We went through a period of time where I was spending 90 percent of my time working with a client that was about 5 or 10 percent of our revenue, just trying to collect. Now we want business from the Fortune 500 companies, so we go after those aggressively.

I joined 100 Black Men in 1994. I needed to be around a group of men like Sam and others who are leaders in this community, from both a business standpoint and a social standpoint. They were leaders in this community in terms of trying to impact the lives of African American boys in this city. After joining 100 Black Men, I once went on a trip with Sam to South Carolina. He opened up and began to talk, and we became friends. I started following him, tracking his footsteps.

He went to the Chamber of Commerce as the chairman. I was at the 100 Black Men Christmas dinner one night and I asked, "Sam would you put me on the board of the chamber?" He said, "Yeah, I would do that for you," so I followed Sam to the chamber.

The next chamber president was Tommy Frist, and I became friends with him. Then Sam said, "Well, I need to get you involved with Senator Frist's campaign. I need you to contribute two thousand dollars." Quite frankly, as an African American, I voted Democrat, but I thought it would be a great opportunity to build relationships. If you know Sam, he'll tell you that building relationships is key to growing your business—people do business with people they like and trust. So I contributed the funds and later became friends with the senator. That is just kind of how Sam shows you to make strategic moves that benefit you. One of our clients now is HCA because of my relationship with Tommy Frist.

I followed in Sam's footsteps and became the chairman of 100 Black Men of Middle Tennessee. Senator Frist came last December at a fund-raiser for us, so it is not just getting business for myself but also about helping other folks who are less fortunate. The focus is on the bottom line, but the bottom line is not just about the bottom line. It is about helping this community to become a better place for everybody. A lot of CEOs in this town volunteer at various nonprofits.

About two years ago Sam asked me to participate in his Monday morning session at Tennessee State University. Every fourth Monday of the month, different business people come and share ideas about how they can improve their businesses. Sam would give them insight in terms of marketing, cash flow, P&L, and balance sheet. He recently explained what a balance sheet was, what an income statement was, and what affects them. I don't know if people realize the value of having him sit across the table to analyze their business.

As I said, one piece of key business advice Sam gave me was to work on building relationships. The other one was to avoid marketing my business as a minority business just because I'm an African American. Sam said, "Darrell, you need to market your business as just being a business and throw away the minority piece—not that that is bad, but you need to go after companies just as a business, not as a minority business." That showed me how I was pursuing contracts to get 10 percent of the contract instead of going after the entire contract. Just changing my whole thought process helped me to open up.

So we went from being a minority subcontractor to being a prime contractor, all because of the thinking process. I had stymied the growth of the business by pursuing 10 percent of the opportunity. Once he helped me change the psychology of being just a business, not a minority business, that helped open a lot of doors. I even went out and hired a public relations firm to help transform the image of the company from a minority business to just a business, and that was helpful. But the adjustment in the psychology was more helpful because I'm the CEO, and I had to change not only the way I thought but the way the people in the organization thought.

Because of that, and many other factors, the company has grown tremendously since then. Ten years ago, we had about 8 to 10 employees, now we have 165. We had about $2.5 million in sales, and this year we'll have about $16 million.

Another key bit of advice he gave me: "Darrell, the best time to fire somebody is when you first think about it. It doesn't get any better after then. And also, always have one less person working at your company than is needed."

Sometimes Sam gives me advice even when I don't ask for it. You see, Sam's career is very different from mine. I have been an entrepreneur since I was twenty-six, and Sam worked for someone until he was in his fifties. I think he missed a lot of time raising his children by working in corporate America. He says, "Have dinner with your family every night. They want to know they have an opportunity to sit down and talk with you, to know that you are going to be there." So I always leave work early to get to the soccer field. The kids are priority to me over business. I only have one chance to be a father. This is my only shot.

Just talking to Sam about how busy he was makes me see what I need to do. Sam has done more in business than 99 percent of people in the world will ever do, or will ever get a chance at doing. I mean, look at him now, he's here, in nice offices, living the American dream. Was it a gradual climb? No. It was up and down. And through all the ups and downs, and when the papers were running negative articles about Sam, he still kept his head up high. That was a learning experience for me. When they were writing those articles, he didn't go away and hide. He still went to all of his meetings. He was still the chamber chair. I think people thought he was going to run and hide, and he did the opposite. If something like that ever happens in my career, I know that I am going to be like Sam and I'm going to keep pushing forward.

So often, Sam was the first and only, the way he was the first African American president of the chamber. He brought me on, and I'm going to bring others on. After I joined, we had a situation where never in the history of the chamber had an African American been a VP as part of their paid staff. After several opportunities to hire qualified black VPs passed, I expressed my frustration. I can remember sitting in the meetings with people on the committee and I said, "You know, guys, I have been reading a book called *Fortunes, Fiddles & Fried Chicken*, about the rise of the Nashville business community in the 1800s to now. That book had a picture of the Chamber of Commerce staff in 1899. The chamber staff today looks like it did in 1899. We have to change that." That finally hit home.

The barriers for people of color are not gone. But I know that when I started Zycron I was black. That is not going to change. I know there are going to be additional challenges; I just have to be prepared for them. There may even be times when your color may help you, but there are more cases where it doesn't. You have to take advantage of the cases when it does, and work a little harder when it works against you. I am a pilot, so every now and then when I fly somewhere I am going to have a headwind. For example, I typically hit a headwind when I fly to Memphis, so I plan for that. In running Zycron as a business, I know I am going to have a headwind, and I've just got to plan for that. Does that mean I'm not going to get up and go to Memphis? No. It means I am going to get up earlier in the morning.

Mike Turney
Mama Turney's Pies
Nashville

I met Sam through Darrell Freeman. Darrell was speaking at a men's conference at Mt. Zion Church in Smyrna. I looked at his story as similar to what we had done. He's doing computers, of course, and we are doing pies. But he had gone from nothing to something. And that's the vision that I see with this company. I think the sky is the limit.

You know, I have to thank Mr. Howard because I had been beat up. I had a vision for this business that nobody else could see. I wanted to do things that were out of the norm for a small business, a minority business. Getting the constant flack from these goals wore me down. It hurt my spirit. The enthusiasm and the drive that I had early on for this business were diminished. You have to have that. That is what Mr. Howard has brought back to me. He has renewed that enthusiasm and that drive.

It's still an ongoing process. I think what helped more than anything is when I met Mr. Howard at a Monday night TSU meeting; right away I think he saw my heart and I think I saw his. He trusted me, and immediately I trusted him.

And the timing, once again, was just right, because I got to tell my story and put my heart out there on the table before any of the other people ever got there. Then Mr. Howard said, "What time are you going to be at your shop tomorrow?" And I said, "Well, I will be there at six o'clock like always." And he said, "I will be there at seven." And that just blew me away. He was going to take time out of his schedule to come down here and see what we're doing with this business.

We started this company, my wife and I, in our home about nine and a half years ago out of what a lot of people would consider failure. I was a meat cutter for twenty-eight years. I started cutting meat when I was about sixteen years old, and went into the meat industry and managed several grocery stores.

I had a buddy that had this grandiose idea about starting a barbecue restaurant, so I quit my job and went in business with him. It didn't work out. I had quit a good job managing the meat department of the Piggly Wiggly in Brentwood to go into that business; I had never quit a job before, having had only four jobs in my life; and I was forty years old. I sat at home, looked at my wife, and told her, "I'm a failure."

We were selling a few pies at the barbecue restaurant. I noticed that some people were coming in and they weren't buying barbecue. They were ordering whole pies and slices of pies, and even getting mad when we didn't have the pies.

So, that sparked the idea right there. I asked my wife, "Do you think we might make some money selling the pies?"

She looked at me like, *He's done lost his mind.* But she supported me, saying, "Well, maybe we can."

I picked six places to go, starting with some high-end places. One of the first was Arthur's restaurant in the Union Station. Another one was the Greasy Spoon, and on the lower end was Dan's Grill on Eighth Avenue. And out of the six places that day, I sold 50 percent of what I went after. Three of those places bought the pies. The chef at Arthur's didn't buy them, but he loved them. I think if I had been more professional with my presentation, if he had thought that I could have handled his supply and demand, he would have bought the pies because he loved it. It was a great pie.

I got home and I said, "I got 50 percent of what I went after today, even though it wasn't but three places." And that's when God kind of birthed the vision in my mind of the business. I said, "If I could get 50 percent of the convenience stores, restaurants, barbecue pits, hospitals, nursing homes, just in the Nashville area, maybe we can make some money out of selling this product."

Now we're all over the state of Tennessee, into Kentucky, the lower end of Indiana, and close to Chicago. We sell pies through Mitchell's Grocery Corporation out of Alabama and Tennessee, in about 300 independent grocery stores; we have the Memphis zone of Kroger stores, which is about 140 stores; we sell through Associated Wholesale Groceries out of Nashville and Memphis, which is approximately around 300 stores; plus we sell through several small distributors such as convenience stores.

Mr. Howard and I reviewed our business with Kroger. It's about 45 percent of our current business, but at one time Kroger was about 60 or 70 percent. What I know in my heart is that we have to continue to diversify the business. We don't have a written contract with Kroger. By the grace of God, we have a product that is good enough that the supply and demand of customers has made them keep buying that product (so far).

We did $689,000 in business in 2003. This year we should do about $800,000–$900,000. Sam says we will do over $1 million.

Sam has helped me with a five-year plan and he's helping me achieve some order. We're working on a presentation for my banker so we can grow this business. There was previously only one day a week that I wasn't baking pies. Sam has helped me to understand that when you have done all you can do, you should just stand back and the Spirit will take care of you.

Sam's helped me understand that I need to be proactive about some issues, so I had a talk with the guys that did the baking. I told them, "You got to get this done because I have a new attitude about this thing. If you're walking around here eating up time and not working, then you are not going to be here." I made a point to bring three interviewees right in front of the workers to let them know how serious I was. The day after that happened, after I talked to the guys, it was a whole new atmosphere in that shop.

The bakers work hard in extremely hot conditions with a 475-degree, room-sized pie oven and a 275-degree pie shrink-wrapping tunnel in the space of a twelve- to thirteen-hundred-square-foot building. They're doing that from three o'clock in the morning to ten or eleven o'clock in the morning. That's a thin line to walk. You can't tell someone who's been up since three o'clock, who is also working two jobs, "Okay, you got to start doing better or else I'm going to fire you." But you have to get this done. If they are not going to do the job, you have to find somebody else who will, but there's a way to do it.

Sam showed me, rather than told me. I know that he has seen some things that I should have already been doing, but he told me to quit beating up on myself about them. So, in turn, the encouragement and the patience that Sam has had with me, I have to pass on to others.

One of the main things Sam told me is not to be discouraged about what people don't believe in or what they can't see because it's ultimately my vision for this business. It's a vision that God gave me, and everybody is not going to see it, not even my wife.

Sam has also taught me to be sure to pay myself a salary, so I can accumulate some money in this business. I had been paying myself, but it has not been as disciplined. I hadn't been paying myself if the money wasn't there. Sometimes, Sam told me, I should pay myself then wait. I need to pay myself every time, even if I have to hold the check for a while.

What has hurt me was priding myself in being a man of my word but having to put people off and say, I really can't pay you this right now. I'm waiting on this and then I can do it. That is bothersome for me, but I know that I have to do this for now to keep this business alive. Right now, I have almost fifty thousand dollars worth of purchase orders in-house that will be filled within the next three weeks. So, what I have to do now is push some of them back, stagger them where I can get them filled, and it can be done. It can be done.

Sam's helped me a lot by just saying, "Do what you're motivated to do—do it, don't fret, just focus, execute. Don't sit there and cry. Just execute. Do all you can do today, go home and get some sleep, come back tomorrow morning."

That saying right there is the one that stuck in my mind. The first day I met Mr. Howard, that's what he told me: "Do all that you can do today and then start over again tomorrow."

I want to be sure I make one last point: The people see Mike Turney all the time with the pies. I want people not to forget that my wife has been so important in all this. Sam says she probably needs to come in about once a week, just to walk through the shop. I know that's right. The pies are always better when Mama Turney is there.

Teresa Evetts Horton
Former Executive Director, Nashville Convention Center
Nashville

I worked with Sam a long time at the convention center, twelve or thirteen years, from the time it was built. When we started, Sam was vice chairman and Tom Irwin was chairman. I was in metro government personnel. They hired Sandra Carl as executive director.

Sandra opened the center as marketing director. Then she became director and ran it. After she went to California, another director came on, for only eight months. He could not stand the politics. After he left, Sam and the others had to beg me to take it because it wasn't as easy as it sounds.

We opened the center in January of '87. Sam and I had been working together two years prior to that. I didn't understand why until I got there, but all of a sudden it dawned on me, *Gosh, I guess they did need me.* Starting a new government agency from scratch with no building, no services, no systems—they did need somebody to help put all that together.

I was doing all the financial stuff, recruiting the staff, making all the purchases. And, of course, it's government, so you have to write all the bid invitations. On top of that, we were trying to put together a staff, which was hard. Sandra had worked in convention centers, but I hadn't, so I was being trained from the beginning. But I had the basic qualities to do the job.

That's where Sam came in at the beginning. He and I hit it off. When I look back, I always think that he saw I needed his help. I always say that he programmed me. He saw that I didn't have any corporate experience. I had been in government since I was twenty, so I had no idea what it was like to work at a private enterprise. Yet they wanted the convention center to be run somewhat like a corporation, but of course, we had to run it as government, too. He had to teach me the corporate side. He always drilled into me how to put the financial reports together. He taught me the lingo, the accounting terms.

I hadn't had Accounting 101, and here I was putting together a company. So, I needed somebody who had done that before. When I would present it wrong, nobody ever knew because before it was made public, he would look at it. He never said, "This is wrong." He would just say, "Let's try it this way." I didn't know I was wrong until he redid the whole thing. That is how we started out.

From that point, he felt that trust from me and I felt like I could trust him. I could talk to him. And with boards, if you don't have a person on the board, especially one as large as ours—ours was thirteen members—you are really in trouble because you need the support of that one person to steer you through board politics.

There is usually somebody on the board that helps you understand how to approach all the different board members and how to make presentations appeal to their different personalities. Sam did this for me.

Sometimes, I could see I wasn't getting my message across. There were thirteen of them and I saw this look in their eyes and I thought, *Are they understanding what I'm saying?* So, I would go back to Sam and ask, "Am I effective?" He would say, "Well, you might want to do this . . . " He did that for me all the time until I got comfortable.

I had never made a board presentation. I had never run a building. I had never experienced anything like that. I always had management taking care of me; I had not been in management. I really started from scratch. And if I had not had the support of people like Sam, I could not have survived.

My life is so full now. I was thinking on the way over here, trying to resurrect some memories of Sam. He was instrumental in my career. I always mention him when I'm talking to any reporter about the people who helped me get where I am today.

There are some little things he doesn't even remember— like the time I had to do my budget presentation for the city council. The finance director and chairman of the board would come to support me. It was all televised.

And I forgot my glasses. I can't read without my glasses.

We were sitting back in the chamber and I was getting ready to go up. I said, "Sam, I forgot my glasses." He looked at me and he said, "You know this stuff." I said, "But this is next year's proposed budget—it's pages and pages of numbers." He said, "You know it, and if you don't know it, just act like you know it." And that was probably the first time that I did that, and I did great.

When it was over, he said, "You put your personality into it. You did better without your glasses because you tend to read your stuff, and everybody is bored to death because that piece of paper is your crutch." I'll never forget him saying that to me. I think about that today.

There were some scary moments. After I took the director's position, the board talked about bringing in private management. In other words, they wanted to hire someone to do my job, to run the convention center. Sam got up to give the commission a little speech.

I didn't know he was going to do that; he never told me. He just started his speech. Harriet is my assistant, and she is close to Sam, too. She has been working with me since she was eighteen and had just graduated from high school. She is now forty-six. We've been together since we were kids. I was twenty-four when I started working with her. So, she's like radar. She knows what I'm thinking and hands me a piece of paper if I'm thinking about that piece of paper. She is just that way. So the board meetings are usually just a piece of cake for us, because we know what each other's thinking.

So Sam just all of a sudden that day takes off. Harriet looked at me like, *What do I do?* At the end of his presentation, he asks the board, "Why would we want to bring in private management when we've got her?" I'll never forget that. I was so proud. The board voted to not even consider it.

That was a key moment because private management hasn't been discussed ever again since Sam did that presentation.

There were other difficult times. After he got the board off private management, then I had to come in and make the proposal to lay off 25 percent of the staff. They said, "Why do we need to do that?" I explained that it was in order to save because the fund didn't look good. They didn't realize that I was looking five and ten years out. I had learned that from Sam already; today is important, but you need to figure out what is going to be happening, if you can, five or ten years from now. I had to look at that with Sam many, many, many days. I said, "We're not going to make it; there's not going to be enough money in here." The board had charged me to never go to the city and ask for subsidy. So I said, "Well, the only way I'm going to be able to do that is to save a million dollars." They said, "How are you going to save a million dollars?" I said, "I don't know, but you are going to have to give me three years."

It was the toughest decision I had to make that year. I came in with the proposal to cut staff, and the board supported me and I executed it. That was when I really became executive director.

I'm going to retire in December. I have been working since I was twenty, for thirty-three years. I have five children. I have seven grandchildren, getting ready to have another one in March. That's pretty amazing when I say it like that. But I'm moving on to a new phase of my life.

HOWARD'S LAW: RULES FOR WORK

A good name is better than all the riches in the world.

—Proverbs 22:1 (paraphrase)

*M*y mother's belief is truer today than ever before. Nothing will put you out of business faster than cheating people or cutting corners. Word gets around.

I'm glad to say, the opposite also seems to be true. Despite all the bad publicity I've had, I haven't lost many friends. They must know me well enough not to believe everything they read.

Having a good name means being honest in all things, even when you think no one is looking. Honesty becomes a habit. The reverse is also true. Padding your expense account with the taxi ride you didn't take, or the breakfast you didn't enjoy, can become addictive. Getting away with it may encourage you to take greater risks; yet, it's so detrimental to your personal development.

That's especially true for black executives. When you get through the door, you stand alone and visible. Think of the multitude of brothers and sisters coming behind you. They will need your shoulders to step on in order to continue our progress. You must be above reproach and squeaky clean.

1. **Surround yourself with positive people with can-do attitudes, and remove those whose limitations are holding back your company.**

   If an employee doesn't share your vision, lead him to the door. You need to work with people who are dedicated to making things work for you, and for your customer.

2. **Hold your staff accountable.**

   Your staff is a reflection of your own work. If one person's performance isn't up to snuff, it will affect the performance and well-being of others. You may have made an inaccurate match of personnel to the task. No matter how the problems occurred, if the situation cannot be fixed, you must fire those who are holding back the company.

3. **The best time to fire somebody is when you've made the decision to do it.**

   Of course, you shouldn't react impulsively to any situation. But once you've made your decision to let someone go, it doesn't get any easier as time goes on. The situation will not improve on its own. Do what you need to do and move on.

4. **Always have one less person working at your company than is really needed.**

   The alternative—having more people than you need—is a recipe for indolence and playtime on your dime. It sets a bad example for others. Having one less person than you need forces people to learn to do each other's jobs. This is good for both your company's efficiency and your employees' growth.

5. **There is no traffic on the extra mile.**

   This was our slogan at Xantus. If you go the extra mile to provide service to your customers, you'll notice that you're out there by yourself. Your customer will notice and come back to you. Do more than your competitors, and you will engender loyalty; customers don't forget.

6. **Don't leave when your staff has to work late. Stay and work alongside them until the job is done, then you can all go home at the same time.**

Being an executive doesn't mean you just crack the whip, give the orders, and then go home. If your staff sees you working, they will roll up their sleeves too. They'll believe in you. Then, during those times when you can't be there, everyone will still work because they know you're not slacking. They'll know that if it were possible, you would be right there with them.

7. **The "25 Percent" Rule.**

If you work 25 percent harder than your competitor, you'll win. Most people work an average of forty hours a week. If you came in one hour earlier and worked one hour later, you'd spend 25 percent more time at your task than most. If you did that every day, you'd be 25 percent ahead, get 25 percent more done, and have 25 percent better success.

Without the additional 25 percent, you're just average. Remember, if you're doing nothing, you're never finished.

8. **If you want to be an entrepreneur, take your first job in a big corporation to learn what you can do.**

Don't expect to graduate from school and start making deals. You'll have to learn the ropes first, and as Aristotle said, "We learn by doing." It's best if you can learn by doing on someone else's dime. I learned most of the intricacies of doing business not at college or graduate school or even as a White House fellow, but by making deals and acquisitions with brilliant mentors like Jack Anderson, my boss at HAI, and by ironing out financial problems at Meharry Medical College.

9. Take all opportunities offered to you.

Don't turn down relocations in the early years of your career. You must demonstrate that you're willing to play the corporate game. Seize any opportunity to learn more about the company and its business entities.

10. Once you decide to go out on your own, focus.

You must be singularly focused in business, rather than trying to be all things to all people. You should be able to state your goals in one simple sentence, and your main goal should be to satisfy a given demand.

11. Think big.

If you have an idea, make sure it's a big one. It takes as much work to make one million dollars as it does to make one hundred thousand.

12. Don't let small stuff keep you from big goals.

If you're going to do business with someone, read the contract; but don't get too hung up on the details. The important thing is to agree you're going to do business together. You'll probably have to rework the details as the deal goes through anyway. Who you do business with is more important than the contract you sign. And once you start talking about drawing up a contract . . .

13. Always offer to prepare the first draft.

I still use this rule, which I learned from Arthur Goldberg at the United Nations in 1966. Many people are lazy. If you always volunteer to do the work, there is a chance you might be taken advantage of . . . but you will often be appreciated, and you will always have a place at the table. Plus, if you write the first draft of any contract, you'll have the first say in what your role will be.

14. When people speak ill of you, they're probably speaking for the benefit of their constituents. Don't take it personally.

Another lesson gleaned from Arthur Goldberg. It helps to understand the politics of business.

15. Have a good and pleasing personality.

No entrepreneur is an island; you will need the goodwill and cooperation of others. Be dependable. You must work to get ahead, but you must also be willing to work with and for others to achieve a position in corporate America. Make others appreciate being around you. Do not be abrasive, sarcastic, rude, or late.

16. Control your ego.

Maintain a low profile. Stay out of marches and controversies, restrain the need to be publicly recognized.

17. Participate in community organizations.

Demonstrate your willingness to serve others to the community-at-large and really put your heart into it. Whether it's the Junior Chamber of Commerce, United Way, or some other nonprofit community agency, your work won't go unnoticed.

18. "Casual Friday" means casual workday.

"Business casual," acceptable in many companies, usually means a less professional appearance. A less-than-professional appearance leads to a less-than-professional attitude. This attitude will be communicated to your clients and staff and through your work. Your clothes and demeanor are your means of expressing your work and product in the business world.

19. Never ask someone to be your mentor.

Carry yourself so that people will want to look up to you and to get on your bandwagon. Do good work and people will want to help you. Accept that help, but don't become dependent on it. Mentors are very important in teaching you the ways of business, but eventually your mentor will leave, retire, or die. You must learn to make your own way.

20. Don't dress better than your boss.

Don't drive a more luxurious car than he or she does, either. You might make the boss jealous, thereby limiting your chances of success. (I never bought a luxury car until I left HCA.)

Always avoid consuming alcohol on business trips, especially with your boss.

21. Don't ask for a raise.

Your toughest negotiations should take place when you have the most strength—when you're offered the job. Once you take the job, you should be rewarded when your work is recognized. If you're making your goals but you're not compensated accordingly, start looking around for the next opportunity.

If it's clear that a job won't take you where you want to go, move on. Don't allow your career to languish because of external circumstances. Take control.

22. Don't play the race card.

If you are a member of a minority, race discrimination exists against you, and it will probably continue through the rest of your life. You must practice strategies that put your professionalism above your racial identity.

The fact is, playing the race card rarely works. Most often, only the lawyers win. Use it only as a very last resort. Carefully weigh the benefits of winning by playing the race card against your chances of corporate success afterwards. If you find race to be a problem in a company, move on.

Race politics in the business world rarely work to the benefit of the victims of discrimination. Consider—one of the largest racial-bias settlements, against Texaco, was $176 million. Where did the money go? The breakdown was as follows: $26 million went to salary increases to current employees; $35 million went to forming a five-year task force to determine and oversee problems in Texaco's personnel policies; $86 million went to 1,340 former and current employees—an average of $60,000 per employee, based on seniority; and $29 million went to legal fees.

The six plaintiffs shared $800,000. The first two collected $200,000 each, and the four who joined later received $100,000 each.

Those six plaintiffs received a small amount of money for what now seems to be a very limited opportunity for success. Some good was achieved, but it was at a very great cost to the six plaintiffs. Their careers have been capped.

I've had some personal experience with a suit that was filed against O'Charley's Restaurants. I serve on that corporate board and was appointed by the federal judge to oversee the implementation of the settlement. Current employees shared $704,797 in stock and cash; former employees shared $1,362,500; the five plaintiffs took home only $129,896, (or around $26,000 each); and applicants who were turned away from O'Charley's took a total of $148,000. The lawyers, however, enjoyed a $2.3 million fee, or half the settlement.

In my opinion, such suits are often an expression of the politics of advocacy. These lawyers use African Americans to enrich themselves at the expense of our credibility. And the awards are not really aiding our cause of fairness under the law.

23. No entrepreneur is an island.

Even if you enjoy flying solo, you'll encounter less wind resistance in a flock. If you're going to get rich, someone else needs to get rich too. Cultivate partners. However . . .

24. Hang on to the biggest interest of your business venture.

You need to make timely decisions, which is difficult if your business is run by committee. And if you're putting the most work into your company, you want the biggest reward.

25. You learn the most from failure.

You may envision yourself a great success when there are no problems along the way. But when adversity strikes, you may despair. Anyone who is a success knows that you will never even learn the meaning of the word "success" unless you have also tasted failure. How else will you improve your methods if you don't fail and have to change them? Every tragedy has a lesson for you, your business, or your life.
  I can tell you that from personal experience.

26. Put God first.

Develop and practice a deep spiritual base, no matter what your roots. Let the Creator guide your success. Learn to listen to this higher power. You may find that your spirit leads you into greater personal success than you had ever dreamed possible.

27. Persevere.

There is no high achievement or destiny without perseverance. One should not grumble about life . . . just plug on. For the victory goes not to the swiftest, but to the one who perseveres.
  For as writer James Russell Miller said:

> It is not enough to begin; continuance is necessary. Mere enrollment will not make a scholar; the pupil must continue in the school through

the long course, until he masters every branch. Success depends upon staying power. The reason for failure in most cases is lack of perseverance.

Especially important: Don't give up five minutes before the miracle.

28. If a business venture depends on politics, wait until the situation is clearly defined before you invest.

TennCare taught me one of my most painful lessons: Politics and business are different. Constituents can sometimes demand—and win—more than paying customers. And politicians will answer to their constituents, no matter how crucial your company is to achieving their stated goals.

29. Spend some time trying to keep this free enterprise system functioning well.

Industrialist Enders M. Voorhees once said:

America is the land of, and for, uncommon men, not only because it affords free choice and opportunity for people to become expert in their chosen occupations, but also because it has mechanisms and incentives for providing the tools of production that the skilled must operate if their skill is to have full fruition in abundant production.

We must, as businesspeople, be diligent in preserving this system of free enterprise. The free enterprise system—with private property, economic freedom, decentralized decision-making, price incentive systems, and restricted role of government in economic matters—means a better society both economically, and in my opinion, socially. Not a perfect society . . . a better society, with adequate flexibility and automatic corrective forces to keep improving the standard of living and individual satisfaction for the constituents: people.

If we want an environment in which small business can succeed, we must, in addition to working in our own businesses, help maintain our excellent economic climate. We must work to preserve it. Be wary of laws that purport to do good for some at the expense of the freedom of business. These laws will ultimately lead to the destruction of the free enterprise system.

30. Do what you can do, then go home and relax. Start again the next day.

If you're putting in an extra 25 percent, you're already ahead of the game. Don't worry about everything at the office once you're at home. Be with your family; enjoy your community. When you know you've done all you can do, you can go home and relax. Get some sleep. You'll be surprised at how much better things may look in the morning.